TM 9-759

WAR DEPARTMENT MANUAL

M4 SHERMAN
MEDIUM TANK
TECHNICAL MANUAL

BY WAR DEPARTMENT

WAR DEPARTMENT · 4 AUGUST, 1942

WAR DEPARTMENT

TECHNICAL MANUAL

MEDIUM TANK M4A3

AUGUST 4, 1942

TECHNICAL MANUAL }
No. 9-759 }

WAR DEPARTMENT
Washington, August 4, 1942

MEDIUM TANK M4A3

Prepared under the direction of
the Chief of Ordnance
(with the cooperation of the Ford Motor Company)

CONTENTS

MEDIUM TANK M4A3

Section I

INTRODUCTION

1. PURPOSE AND SCOPE.

TM 9-759 dated August 4, 1942, is intended to serve temporarily (pending the publication of a revision now in preparation which will be wider in scope) to give information and guidance to the personnel of the using arms charged with the operation and maintenance of this materiel.

2. CONTENT AND ARRANGEMENT OF THE MANUAL.

Sections I through V contain information chiefly for the guidance of operating personnel. Section VI contains information intended chiefly for the guidance of personnel doing maintenance work.

3. REFERENCES.

Section VII lists all Standard Nomenclature Lists, Technical Manuals, and other publications for the material described herein.

Section II

DESCRIPTION AND TABULATED DATA

Paragraph

4. DESCRIPTION (figs. 1 and 2).

a. The medium tank M4A3 is an armored, full track-laying vehicle, powered by a 500 hp Ford tank engine which is an eight cylinder, liquid cooled, "V" type engine designed specifically for tanks. The engine is located in the rear of the hull. The operator steers the vehicle by means of two levers located in the front end of the hull. The vehicle has five forward speeds and one reverse. The tank is wired for radio installation, and for an interphone system within the tank.

b. The turret armor front is 3 inches thick, sides are 2 inches thick, and rear is 2 inches thick. The top of the turret is 1 inch thick. The armor on the sides of the hull is 1½ inches thick and the front slope is 2 inches thick.

c. The turret can be rotated through 360 degrees by a hydraulic system or by hand. The turret platform rotates with the turret.

d. An auxiliary electrical generating system, consisting of a generating set powered by a one-cylinder two-cycle gasoline engine, charges the batteries when the engine generator is not operating.

5. TABULATED DATA.

a. General

Weight without armament, fuel or crew...................................59560 lb
Ground clearance ....17⅜-in.
Tread (center to center of tracks)...83-in.
Width over-all ....103-in.
Length over-all ....232½-in.
Height over-all ....111¾-in.

b. Engine

Ford tank engine
Rated horsepower..500 at 2600 rpm
Number of cylinders (60°V)..8
Weight of engine, w/accessories..1470 lb

c. Armament

1 gun, 75-mm, M3 (combination turret mount)
1 gun, machine, cal. .30, M1919A4 (combination turret mount)
1 gun, machine, cal. .30, M1919A4
     (flexible—ball mount in front plate)

MEDIUM TANK M4A3

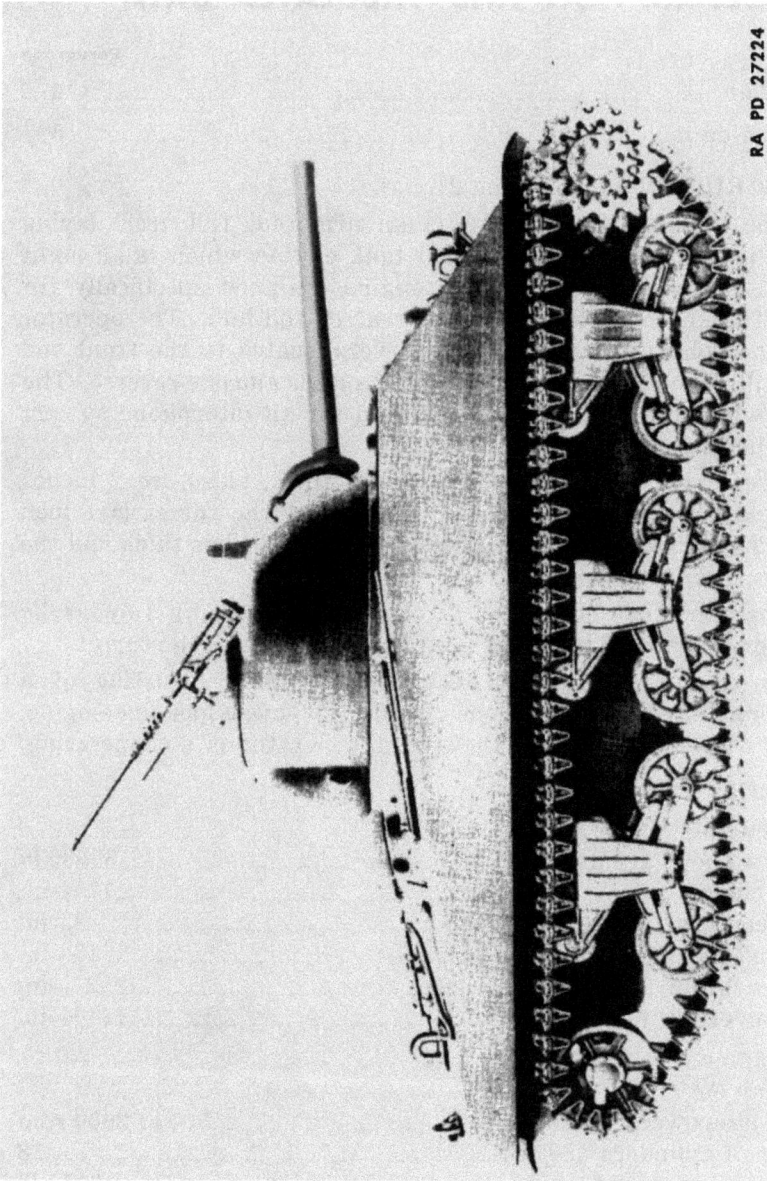

RA PD 27224

Figure 1 — Right Side Medium Tank M4A3

DESCRIPTION AND TABULATED DATA

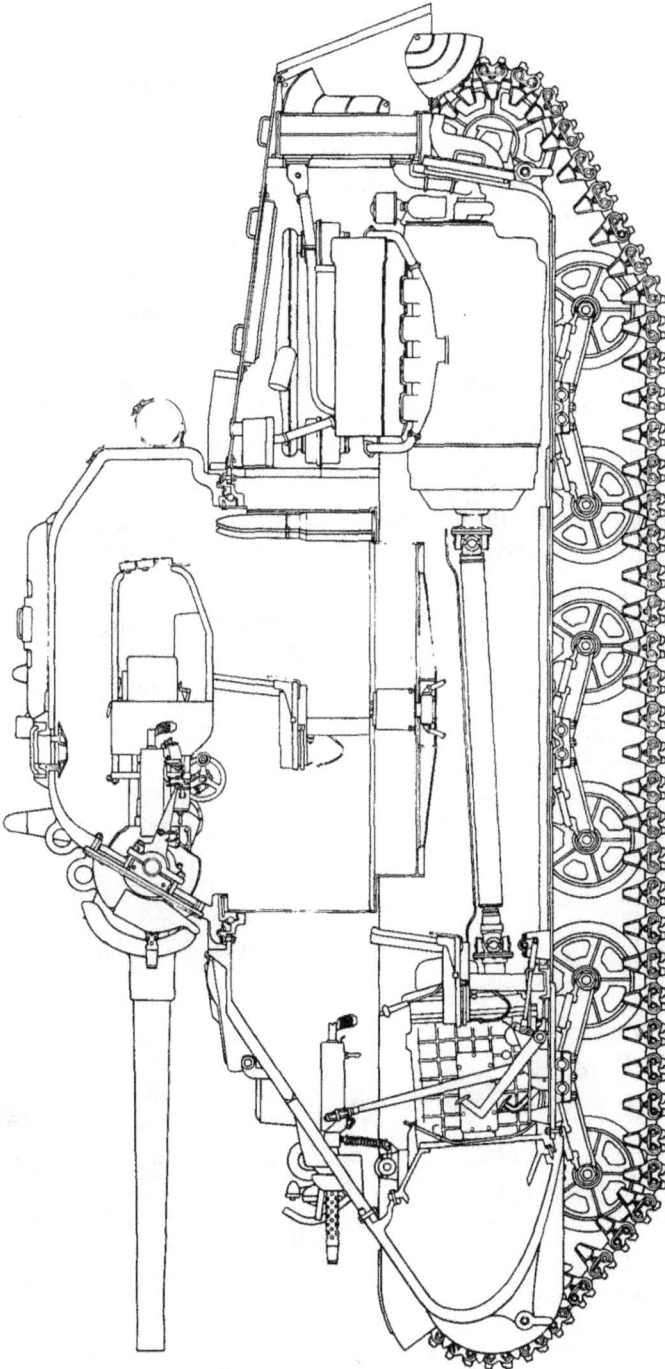

RA PD 27198

Figure 2 — Longitudinal Sectional View Medium Tank M4A3

MEDIUM TANK M4A3

1 gun, machine, cal. .50 M2, H.B.
  (flexible—race mount on turret hatch)
1 gun, submachine, cal. .45 Thompson, Model 1928A1
  (carried on brackets within tank)
1 mount, tripod, machine gun, M1928A1, cal. .30 M2

d. Protected vision. Protected vision is provided for the driver and crew by the use of steel shutters (open and shut type) at vision slots, and by indirect vision devices called periscopes. There are five periscopes on the M4A3 tank. The periscopes for the assistant driver and the gunner are telescope equipped. The remaining three periscopes are of the plain vision type.

e. Seats. Adjustable, padded, chair-type seats, equipped with safety belts, are provided for driver, assistant driver, and gunner. Round, padded seats, equipped with safety belts and of the snap down type, are provided for the loader and tank commander.

f. Protective Padding. Parts of the interior are padded with sponge rubber, to protect the tank crew from injury.

g. Communication

(1) Radio.. { SCR 245 sending and receiving
{ Voice 15-25 miles
{ Code 30-45 miles

(2) Telephone ....Intra-tank

h. Armor thickness

Hull, front slope	2-in.	Bottom, front	1-in.
Rear	1½-in.	Bottom, rear	½-in.
Sides	1½-in.	Turret, front	3-in.
Top	¾-in.	Sides and rear	2-in.
		Top	1-in.
		Rear	2-in.

i. Turret. Cast armor plate...................................360° traverse

j. Fuel and oil

Full capacity ....174 gal
Number of miles without refueling............... { Cross country 110 miles
{ Highway   155 miles
Octane rating of fuel..80 or higher
Engine oil capacity..32 qts
Lubricants...................................See Lubrication Chart

k. Performance

Maximum sustained speed on hard road........................26 mph
Expected cross-country speeds for various terrains..........4 to 26 mph
Maximum allowable engine speed...............................2800 rpm
Minimum engine idling speed.................................500 rpm

DESCRIPTION AND TABULATED DATA

Maximum grade ascending ability...27°
Maximum grade descending ability...27°
Maximum width of ditch tank will cross.......................................72-in.
Maximum vertical obstacle such as a wall, that the tank
   will climb over...18-in.
Maximum fording depth (at slowest forward speed)..................36-in.

   l. Crew ....5 men

   m. Tracks ....rubber block or steel
Track shoe width...16-in.
Track pitch ....6-in.

Section III

OPERATING INSTRUCTIONS AND CONTROLS

6. GENERAL INFORMATION ON CONTROLS (figs. 3 and 4).

a. Spark control. The spark control is entirely automatic and requires no attention by the operator of the vehicle.

b. Throttle controls. A foot throttle pedal is located on the floor in front of the driver's seat, convenient to the driver's right foot. In conjunction with the foot pedal, a hand-operated throttle is provided, which is bracket mounted to the differential case above the foot throttle.

c. Steering levers. Two steering levers are mounted on the floor of the vehicle, in front of the driver's seat. To steer the vehicle, pull the steering lever on the side toward which it is desired to turn. Pulling back either one of the levers slows down the track on that side, while the the speed of the other track is increased. Thus the vehicle turns with power on both tracks at all times (fig. 3).

d. Brakes.

(1) **Service brakes.** Pulling back simultaneously on both steering levers slows down or stops the vehicle, depending on the effort applied.

(2) **Parking brake.** The parking brake lever is located on the right side of the driver, at rear of the transmission. **It is a transmission type brake, and should never be used for any purpose other than parking.** Always be sure parking brake is released before moving the tank.

e. Clutch. The clutch pedal is located on the floor in front of driver's seat, convenient to the driver's left foot. To permit shifting of gears, the clutch is disengaged by depressing the clutch pedal.

f. Utility outlet. Two utility outlets are provided at the top of the instrument panel that permit plugging in trouble light, windshield wiper, etc.

g. Light switches. The knob on the instrument panel marked "LIGHTS" controls the service lights and the blackout driving

OPERATING INSTRUCTIONS AND CONTROLS

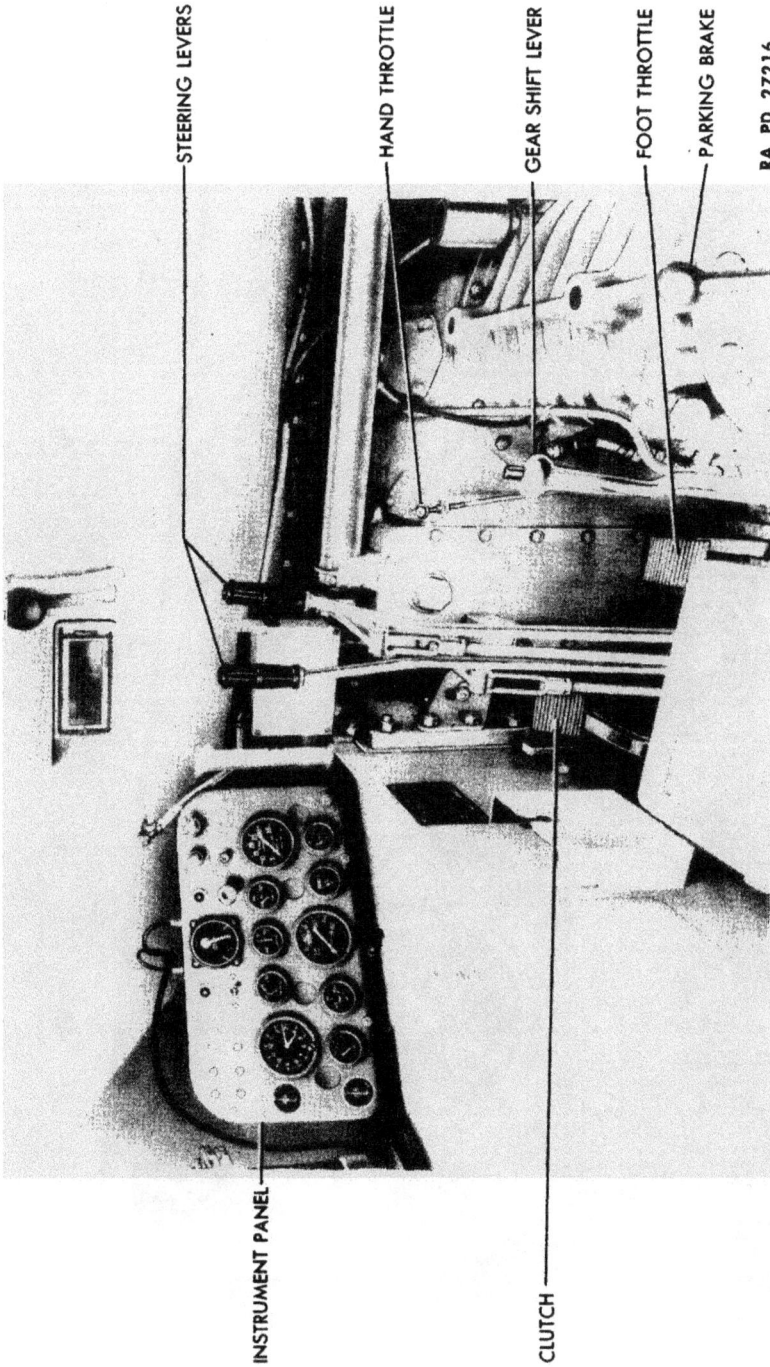

STEERING LEVERS

HAND THROTTLE

GEAR SHIFT LEVER

FOOT THROTTLE

PARKING BRAKE

RA PD 27216

INSTRUMENT PANEL

CLUTCH

Figure 3 – Driver's Compartment

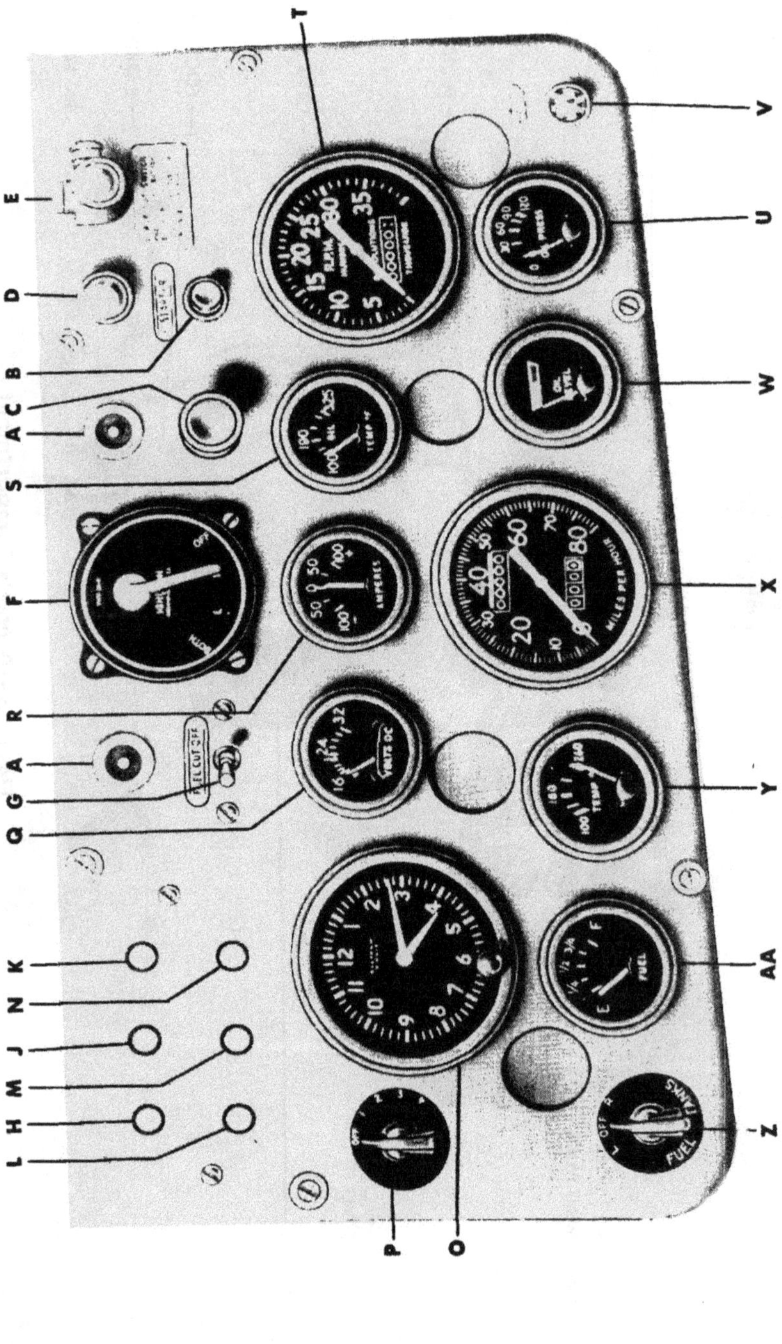

MEDIUM TANK M4A3

Figure 4 — Instrument Panel

RA PD 27217

A—UTILITY OUTLET
B—STARTER BUTTON
C—PRIMER PUMP
D—BLACKOUT DRIVE SWITCH
E—LIGHT SWITCH
F—IGNITION SWITCH
G—FUEL CUT-OFF SWITCH
H—CIRCUIT BREAKER BUTTON —RIGHT HAND UTILITY OUTLET CIRCUIT
J—CIRCUIT BREAKER BUTTON —LEFT HAND UTILITY OUTLET CIRCUIT
K—CIRCUIT BREAKER BUTTON — BLACK-OUT DRIVE SWITCH CIRCUIT
L—CIRCUIT BREAKER BUTTON —SIREN CIRCUIT
M—CIRCUIT BREAKER BUTTON —FUEL CUT-OFF AND HULL LAMPS CIRCUIT

N—CIRCUIT BREAKER BUTTON —CIR-CUIT FOR PANEL LIGHTS, FUEL GAGE, WATER TEMPERATURE, LOW PRESSURE LIGHT, OIL LEVEL GAGE, VOLTMETER, AND TRANSMISSION OIL TEMPERA-TURE GAGE
O—CLOCK
P—PANEL LIGHT RHEOSTAT
Q—VOLTMETER
R—AMMETER
S—TRANSMISSION OIL TEMPERATURE GAGE
T—TACHOMETER
U—ENGINE OIL PRESSURE
V—LOW OIL PRESSURE LAMP
W—ENGINE OIL LEVEL GAGE
X—SPEEDOMETER
Y—ENGINE OIL TEMPERATURE GAGE
Z—FUEL TANK SELECTOR SWITCH
AA—FUEL TANK LEVEL GAGE

RA PD 27217A

Figure 4A—Instrument Panel Nomenclature

11

lights. A spring-operated safety button prevents the knob from being accidentally pulled out beyond the blackout position. To release, push button in with thumb, at the same time continuing outward pull on knob with first and second fingers. The switch has three positions (besides "OFF"), controlling lights as follows: .

Light Switch Position	Lights Operating	Location
Blackout—1st position	Blackout headlights	Top of right and left headlights
	Blackout taillights	Lower section right and left taillights
	Blackout stop light	Upper section right hand taillight
Service—2nd position	Service headlights	Right and left headlights
	Service taillight	Upper section left hand taillight
	Service stop light	Upper section left hand taillight
Stop light—3rd position	Service stop light	Upper section left hand taillight

h. Blackout driving light switch. The blackout driving light may be used to supply illumination for driving when the service driving lights might reveal the position of the tank. First, remove both service headlights from their sockets at the front of the tank. Then insert the blackout driving light in the left front lamp socket. With the master light switch pulled out to first position, pull out on blackout driving light switch button to turn on driving light. The blackout headlight, taillights, and stop light will also be on with switches in this position. CAUTION: Under battle conditions the blackout driving light should be used intermittently and only when absolutely necessary for safe vision.

i. Starter switch. Directly beneath the blackout drive switch a starter button is provided. When pushed in this button completes circuit through the starter switch solenoid closing the starting motor circuit, causing the starter to crank the engine.

j. Primer. A priming pump is provided and located to the left of the starter button. To operate the primer, the button is pulled out and pushed back in. This causes a quantity of gasoline to be forced directly into the intake manifold for cold weather starting. The priming pump is used in place of the conventional choke. Ordinarily it will not be necessary to use the primer except during cold weather.

OPERATING INSTRUCTIONS AND CONTROLS

Excessive priming of the engine will cause flooding and failure to start, and the excess gasoline will wash the oil from the cylinder walls with the result that the cylinder will not be properly lubricated until the engine oil starts circulating.

k. Ignition switch. The Ford tank engine uses two 4-cylinder Bosch magnetos which are controlled by a 4-position switch in the center of the instrument panel at the top. When the switch lever is to the left, both magnetos are on. When the switch lever is at the position marked "L" the left hand magneto only is on, and the engine would be running on the left hand four cylinders. Left or right are used with reference to the engine as viewed from the rear of the tank. When the ignition switch lever is at the position marked "R" the right hand magneto is on and the engine will run on the four cylinders on the right hand bank only.

l. Fuel cut-out. To the left of the ignition switch a spring loaded toggle switch is provided which operates the carburetor degasser electrically. When stopping the engine always pull this toggle switch to the right and hold in this position until the engine stops before turning off the ignition. This shuts off the fuel from the idle fuel supply wells in the carburetor. This will prevent loading up of the carburetor in case the engine is to be restarted while still hot.

m. Circuit breakers. Six circuit breaker buttons are provided in the upper left hand corner of the instrument panel, which control the six circuit breakers which take the place of the conventional fuses. In each instance when these circuits are overloaded, the circuit breaker will open. The circuit involved is then closed merely by pressing the correct button. The circuits controlled by these six buttons are as follows (fig. 4):

(h) Right hand utility outlet circuit

(j) Left hand utility outlet circuit

(k) Blackout drive switch circuit

(l) Siren circuit

(m) Fuel cut-off and hull lamps circuits

(n) Circuit for panel lights, fuel gage, water temperature, low pressure light, oil level gage, voltmeter, and transmission oil temperature gage.

n. Clock. Directly beneath the six circuit breaker buttons an 8-day clock is provided. A reset and rewinding knob is located at the bottom of the dial.

o. Compartment light rheostat. To the left of the clock a 5-position rheostat is provided which controls the brilliance of the panel lights.

p. Voltmeter. To the right of the clock a voltmeter having a range from 16 to 32 volts is provided. When the battery master switch is off, the voltmeter will read at the lower end of the scale. When the master switch is "on," the voltmeter should read battery voltage (approximately 24 volts). If reading is low with the engine not running and no electrical energy is being used, the batteries are low in charge and should be recharged. At normal operating speeds during normal ambient temperatures, the voltage should not exceed 30 volts. If the reading is greater than this, the generator regulator is not properly limiting the voltage, and should be replaced; otherwise the generator will burn out. This voltmeter likewise reads while the auxiliary generating unit is charging the battery, at which time the voltage should not exceed 30 volts.

q. Ammeter. To the right of the voltmeter an ammeter is provided with a range of 100 ampere discharge to 100 ampere charge. If during normal operation when little current is being used, the ammeter consistently indicates discharge either the generator regulator is not functioning properly or the generator itself is at fault. In either case the battery is not being charged and will quickly discharge. These units should receive immediate attention to prevent failure during operation. Even with no electrical energy being used the ammeter should never go above 50 amperes (plus or charge) (100 amperes on tanks having two generators). If the ammeter indicates more than 50 ampere charge, (100 amperes on tanks having two generators) the current limiting unit in the generator regulator is at fault and the regulator should be replaced; otherwise the generator will burn out during operation.

r. Oil temperature gage. To the right of the ammeter an oil temperature gage having a range of from 100 to 325 degrees indicates the temperature of the oil in the transmission.

s. Tachometer. The tachometer is located on the right hand side of the instrument panel to the left of the transmission oil temperature gage. The throttle stop screw on the carburetor should be so adjusted that the engine should idle at 500 rpm after warm-up. The maximum speed of the engine is governed by a flyball type governor located at the rear of the right hand cylinder head. This governor is set to limit the engine speed to 2650 rpm under full load with wide open throttle (10-inch vacuum). If during operation under full load it is possible to run the engine at speeds above 2650 rpm, or if the governor limits the speed at some point below 2650 rpm, the ordnance maintenance personnel will be notified. If the governor is set too low it will be impossible to get maximum speed and power from the vehicle; on the other hand if the governor is set too high, damage to the engine and other working parts could result.

OPERATING INSTRUCTIONS AND CONTROLS

t. Oil pressure gage. An engine oil pressure gage is located directly beneath the tachometer. At normal temperatures the oil pressure should be between 60 and 80 pounds. If during operation the oil pressure suddenly drops off, immediately stop the engine. This fault may be due to low oil level. If oil pressure drops off slowly, it may be due to a change in the viscosity of the oil due to overheating. Check engine temperature.

u. Low oil pressure signals. To the right of the oil pressure gage a red jewel type light is provided that signals the driver when the oil pressure drops below eight pounds.

v. Oil level gage. An oil level gage located between the speedometer and the oil pressure gage indicates whether sufficient oil is carried in the oil pan sump. As long as the oil level gage is in the green sector, the oil level is satisfactory. When the reading drops to the red sector, oil should be added to bring the reading up to the right hand side of the green sector.

w. Speedometer. The speedometer is located in the center of the instrument panel at the bottom, and is equipped with a trip mileage reset at the bottom of the instrument panel.

x. Engine temperature gage. The engine temperature gage is located to the left of the speedometer and is calibrated from 100 to 260 degrees. The cooling system on the M4A3 tank is sealed and not open to atmospheric pressure, with the result that boiling point of the coolant and consequently overheating actually does not occur until a temperature of approximately 230 degrees is reached. In normal operation under maximum power on a level hard surface the engine temperature should not be greater than 90 degrees above atmospheric temperature.

y. Fuel level gage and selector switch. In the lower left hand corner of the instrument panel a selector switch and fuel level gage, permit the checking of the fuel level in the two sponson fuel tanks. The selector switch has three positions "L" (left), "Off," and "R" (right). With the selector switch in the "Off" position the fuel level gage will read "E" (empty). With the selector switch in the left position the fuel level gage will indicate the level of the fuel in the left hand sponson tank. With the selector switch in the "R" position the fuel level gage will indicate the level of the fuel in the right hand sponson tank.

z. Battery master switch (fig. 5). A battery master switch is located approximately 30 inches to the rear of the driver's seat and underneath the turret basket floor. To open or close this switch, it is necessary to raise the knob approximately 1/8-inch and turn. When this switch is open all electrical power is shut off at the battery

MEDIUM TANK M4A3

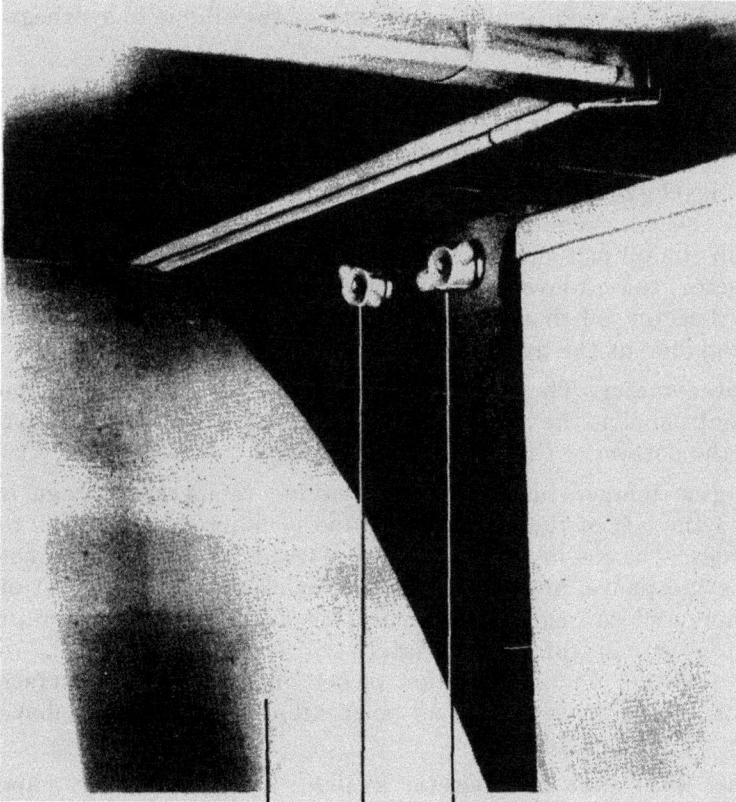

RA PD 27237

TURRET BASKET

RADIO MASTER SWITCH

BATTERY MASTER SWITCH

Figure 5 — Master Switches as Viewed from Driver's Seat

OPERATING INSTRUCTIONS AND CONTROLS

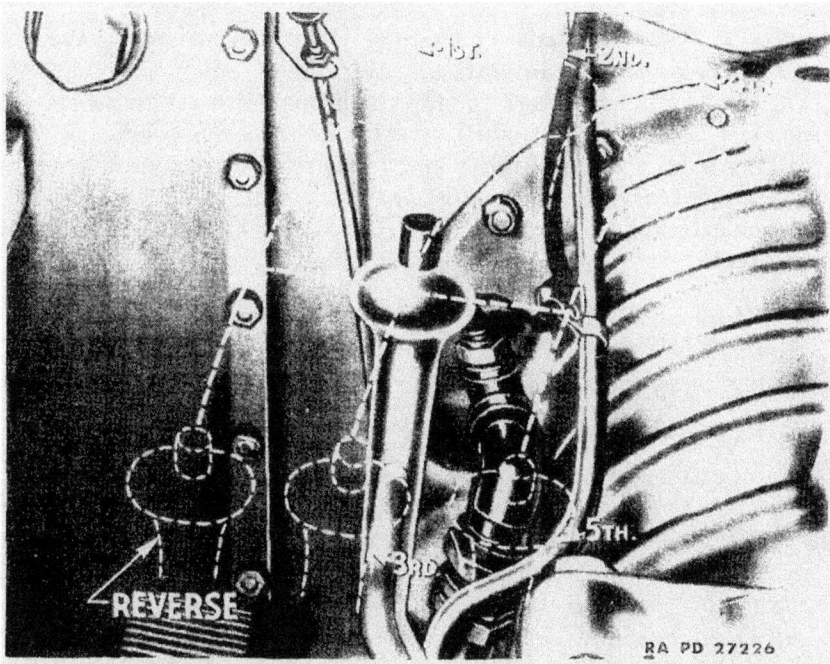

Figure 6 — Gear Shift Lever Positions

(with the exception of the power used by the radio which is controlled by a separate radio master switch). If in doubt as to whether the battery master switch is on, the following can serve as a guide. When the battery master switch is off, the engine temperature gage will read "Full Scale" (260 deg.) and the oil level gage will read at the bottom of the red sector. When the battery master switch is on, the engine temperature gage will indicate the temperature of the coolant in the engine, or if its temperature is below 100 degrees it will indicate 100 degrees, and the oil level gage will indicate the oil level and should be in the green sector.

   aa. **Gear shifting** (fig. 6)

   (1) **Description.** Shifting of gears in the transmission for speed changes is accomplished by the gear shift lever, located on the left side of the transmission, to the right of the driver. The positions of the gear shift lever for the various speeds are shown in figure 6. The gear shift lever is equipped with a latch which prevents accidental shifting into first speed or reverse. The latch must be released by pressing down the button on top of the lever before shifting into first speed or reverse.

   (2) **Operation.** When it is desired to shift to low or reverse, the following procedure will make the shift possible without the clash-

ing of gears which usually results. From neutral move the gear shift lever as though to shift into third gear. Maintain pressure in this direction long enough to stop the propeller shaft and then, with the clutch still held out, shift smartly into low or reverse. If when shifting to any of the higher speeds there is a raking of gears, go back to neutral and, still holding the clutch out, start the shift over. **Do not attempt to complete a shift that begins with a clashing of gear teeth.**

7. PRESTARTING INSPECTION.

Before the engine is started follow procedure outlined under prestarting inspection in Section V.

8. STARTING INSTRUCTIONS.

Before attempting to start the engine, familiarize yourself with all of the various instruments and controls, as outlined in paragraph 6; make sure that the function of each control is thoroughly understood and that the significance of the readings on the various instruments is appreciated.

a. Open gasoline shut-off valves which are located in the left side of the fighting compartment (fig. 7). If the fuel tanks are full, run from right tanks for 30 minutes to provide expansion space for the fuel before opening valves on left fuel tank.

b. Close battery master switch.

c. Put gear shift lever in neutral.

d. Pull hand throttle out about 1/4-inch.

e. In cold weather prime the engine three to nine quick pulls on the primer, depending on outside temperature.

f. Depress clutch pedal.

g. Turn magneto switch to "both" position.

h. Press starter button.

i. Engine should start readily.

9. ENGINE TEST.

a. As soon as the engine starts, check oil pressure. Stop engine if the oil pressure is not indicated in 30 seconds.

b. Check the operation of instruments and switches while the engine is idling. Idle engine until engine temperature gage reads above 100 degrees.

c. When engine is sufficiently warm set hand throttle to 800 rpm. Run the engine on each magneto and compare each tachometer reading with the reading when both magnetos were used. When either magneto shows a drop to less than 400 rpm, the cause should be investigated.

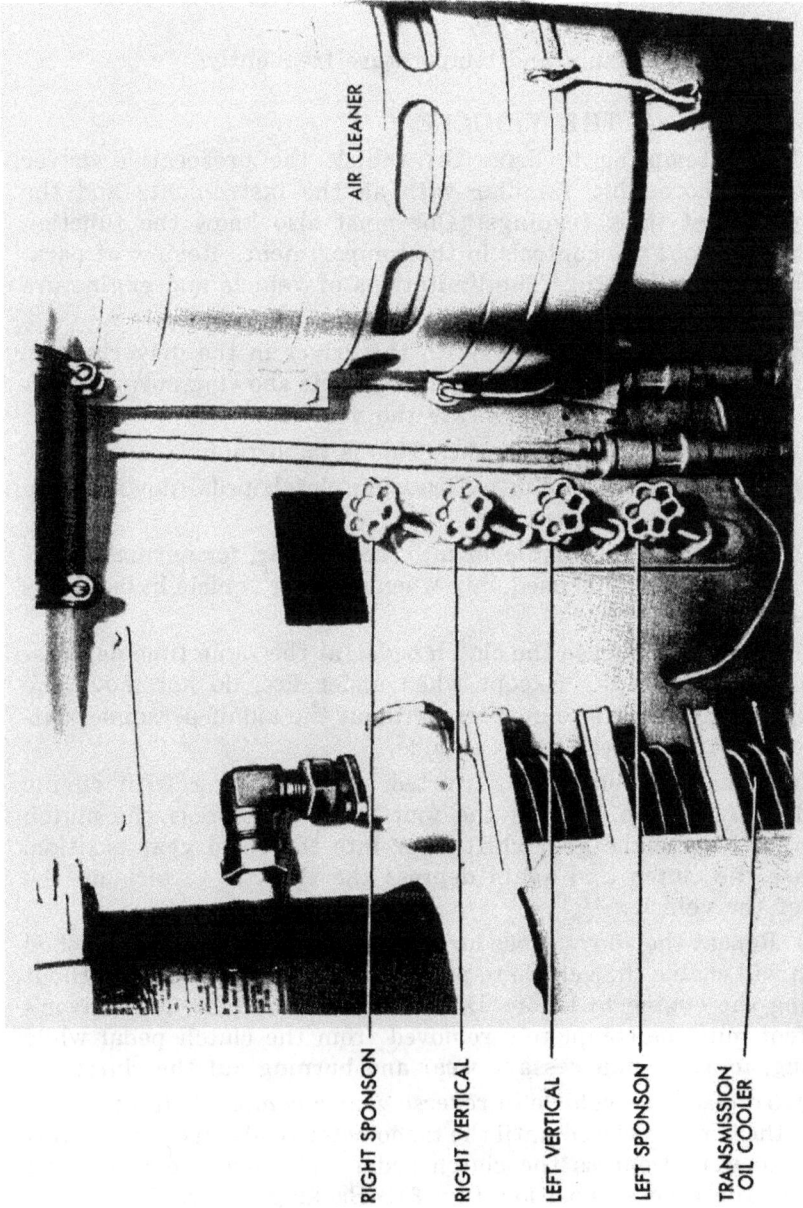

RA PD 27236

AIR CLEANER

RIGHT SPONSON

RIGHT VERTICAL

LEFT VERTICAL

LEFT SPONSON

TRANSMISSION
OIL COOLER

Figure 7 — Left Side Bulkhead—Fighting Compartment

d. Push hand throttle in. (Carburetor stop screws should be set to idle the engine at 500 rpm after warming up.) **Never idle the engine at less than 500 rpm.**

e. Never lug engine below 1000 rpm at wide open throttle. Shift to a lower gear.

f. Check oil pressure and temperature frequently.

10. OPERATING THE VEHICLE.

Before attempting to drive the vehicle the prospective driver should be thoroughly familiar with all the instruments and the significance of their readings. One must also know the function and operation of the controls in the compartment. Review of paragraph 5 will be helpful. The limitations of vehicle and engine are covered under paragraph 4.

a. Operating instructions. With the driver in the driver's seat, the engine at idling speed, and all instruments showing normal readings, the driver may now operate the vehicle.

(1) **Release the parking brake.** This is important.

(2) Disengage the clutch by pressing clutch pedal down to the floor and holding it down.

(3) Move the gear shift lever into second gear, for normal operation. First gear will be used only when shifting vehicle in buildings or over obstacles.

(4) Gradually release the clutch pedal, at the same time depressing the foot throttle. Except when under fire, do not move the vehicle in or out of close quarters without the aid of personnel outside of the vehicle serving as a guide.

(5) When the vehicle has started and is moving with engine speed of 1200 rpm, release the foot throttle, depress the clutch again, and move the gear shift lever into the third gear position. Release the clutch and again depress the throttle to pick up the load of the vehicle.

(6) Repeat the above procedure until the highest gear is reached which will enable the vehicle to proceed at the desired speed without causing the engine to labor. Do not ride the clutch. The driver's left foot must be completely removed from the clutch pedal while driving, **to avoid unnecessary wear and burning out the clutch.**

(7) To place the vehicle in reverse gear a complete stop must be made, the throttle closed until the tachometer reads 500 rpm (lowest idling speed). Depress the clutch pedal and move the gear shift lever to the reverse position (fig. 6). Backing the vehicle should never be attempted unless an observer is stationed in front to guide the driver.

OPERATING INSTRUCTIONS AND CONTROLS

(8) To steer the vehicle pull back the right hand steering lever to make a right turn or the left hand lever for a left turn. This action brakes the track on the inside of the turn and speeds up the outside track. The driver should anticipate each turn and be ready to apply more power as it is needed to compensate for the braking effort. The hands should be free of the steering lever when not actually steering the tank.

(9) To stop the vehicle, release the throttle and pull back on both steering levers at the same time. Depress the clutch pedal when the vehicle has slowed down to approximately two to five miles per hour, depending upon which gear is being employed before stopping. Set the hand throttle for a tachometer reading of 500 rpm for the duration of the halt.

(10) The tachometer, the oil temperature gage, and the oil pressure gage give the most satisfactory indications of the engine's performance. Should the indications of any of these instruments appear to be irregular, the engine should be stopped, and the cause investigated.

b. **Towing instructions:**

(1) **Equipment.** A towing shackle is mounted on each corner of the hull of the vehicle about 20 inches from the ground. Two of these shackles are mounted in front and two in the rear. These shackles provide a quick method of attaching either the "towing bar" or cables.

(2) **Precautions.** If there are tracks on the vehicle to be towed, always disconnect the propeller shaft at the transmission companion flange and leave the vehicle in fifth gear. This procedure insures adequate circulation of the transmission oil while the vehicle is in motion. If the tracks are removed before towing the vehicle, this precaution is not necessary. In towing there are several precautions that the driver must take to avoid trouble or unnecessary delay. Changes of direction are always to be made by a series of slight turns so that the vehicle being towed is as nearly as possible directly behind the one doing the towing or "tracking." This will prevent the cable from contacting the track, which might ruin both the cable and the track blocks. Soft muddy ground is to be avoided, since the tracks may slip on such a surface. If it is necessary to cross a muddy area, the driver should be careful to straighten out both vehicles before entering it, as it is more difficult to pull a tank at an angle than when following in tow. Grousers may be installed as required. The maximum speed when towing should be not more than 12 miles per hour and then only with an operator for steering and braking the towed vehicle. NOTE: Except in cases where a "short hitch"

is absolutely necessary a towing cable will not be coupled to another vehicle by other than the thimbled eyes provided at both ends. Doubling the cable causes sharp bends in the wire rope which will cause rapid failure of the strands and will leave the cable extremely dangerous to handle. When a "short hitch" is desired, the two eyes of the cable are attached to the towing vehicle. The cable with leads **crossed**, is then passed through both shackles of the towed vehicle. This provides an arrangement having a minimum of bending action and movement at the shackles, and furnishes clearance between cable and tracks.

(3) **Method.** If no operator is available to steer the disabled vehicle one cable will facilitate tracking of the towed vehicle. Care must be taken on turning, not to get the cable tangled up with the track of either vehicle.

11. STOPPING THE ENGINE.

After completing a run, the engine must be allowed to operate at 500 rpm for two minutes to assure a gradual and uniform cooling of the valves and other various engine parts.

Section IV

LUBRICATION

12. GENERAL.

The following lubrication instructions for medium tank M4A3 are published for the information and guidance of all concerned, and supersede all previous instructions. Materiel must be lubricated in accordance with the latest instructions contained in Technical Manuals and/or Ordnance Field Service Bulletins.

13. LUBRICATION GUIDE (figs. 8 and 9).

Lubrication instructions for all points to be serviced are shown in War Department Lubrication Guide No. 104, which specifies the types of lubricants required and the intervals at which they are to be applied. The following lubrication instructions contain the same information as the guide. Guides from which data are reproduced are 10x15 in. laminated charts which are part of the accessory equipment of each piece of materiel.

14. POINTS TO BE LUBRICATED BY ORDNANCE MAINTENANCE PERSONNEL.

Generators. Remove and repack generator bearings with GREASE, ball and roller bearing, once each year.

15. REPORTS AND RECORDS.

a. Reports. If lubrication instructions are closely followed, proper lubricants used, and satisfactory results are not obtained, a report will be made to the ordnance officer responsible for the maintenance of the materiel.

b. Records. A complete record of lubrication servicing will be kept for the materiel.

16. LUBRICATION GUIDE NOTES.

Additional lubrication and service instructions on individual units and parts:

1. FITTINGS — Clean before applying lubricant. Lubricate bogie wheels, idler and track support rollers, tachometer and speedometer

MEDIUM TANK M4A3

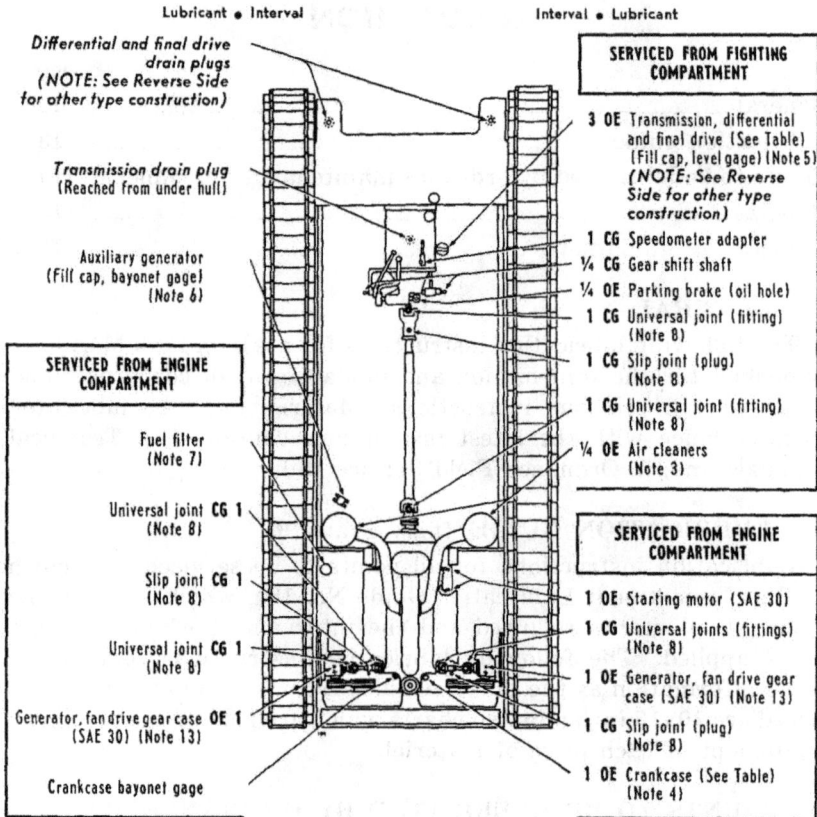

Lubricant • Interval   Interval • Lubricant

Differential and final drive
drain plugs
(NOTE: See Reverse Side
for other type construction)

Transmission drain plug
(Reached from under hull)

Auxiliary generator
(Fill cap, bayonet gage)
(Note 6)

**SERVICED FROM ENGINE
COMPARTMENT**

Fuel filter
(Note 7)

Universal joint **CG 1**
(Note 8)

Slip joint **CG 1**
(Note 8)

Universal joint **CG 1**
(Note 8)

Generator, fan drive gear case **OE 1**
(SAE 30) (Note 13)

Crankcase bayonet gage

**SERVICED FROM FIGHTING
COMPARTMENT**

3 OE Transmission, differential
and final drive (See Table)
(Fill cap, level gage) (Note 5)
(NOTE: See Reverse
Side for other type
construction)

1 CG Speedometer adapter
¼ CG Gear shift shaft
¼ OE Parking brake (oil hole)
1 CG Universal joint (fitting)
(Note 8)
1 CG Slip joint (plug)
(Note 8)
1 CG Universal joint (fitting)
(Note 8)
¼ OE Air cleaners
(Note 3)

**SERVICED FROM ENGINE
COMPARTMENT**

1 OE Starting motor (SAE 30)
1 CG Universal joints (fittings)
(Note 8)
1 OE Generator, fan drive gear
case (SAE 30) (Note 13)
1 CG Slip joint (plug)
(Note 8)
1 OE Crankcase (See Table)
(Note 4)

----- KEY -----

LUBRICANTS	INTERVALS
OE—OIL, engine	¼— 250 MILES
CG—GREASE, general purpose	1—1,000 MILES
No. 1 (above +32°)	3—3,000 MILES
No. 1 or No. 0 (+32° to +10°)	**CHECK DAILY**
No. 0 (below +10°)	Crankcase
	Gear cases
	Air cleaners

Preliminary lubrication instructions based on Pilot model only.

TABLE OF CAPACITIES WITH RECOMMENDATIONS AT TEMPERATURES SHOWN

	Capacity	Above +32°	+32° to +10°	+10° to —10°	Below —10°
Engine Crankcase	32 qt.	**OE** SAE 30	**OE** SAE 30 or 10	**OE** SAE 10	
Trans., Diff. and Final Drives (Single unit)	152 qt.	**OE** SAE 50	**OE** SAE 50	**OE** SAE 50	
Trans. and Diff. (3-piece unit)	64 qt.				
Final Drives (each) (3-piece unit)	36 qt.				

RA PD 27242

Figure 8 — Lubrication Chart on Power Drive Units

LUBRICATION

TANK, MEDIUM, M4A3

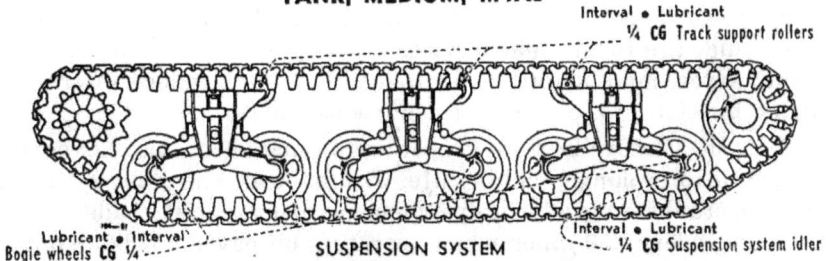

Interval • Lubricant
¼ **CG** Track support rollers

Lubricant • Interval
Bogie wheels **CG** ¼

SUSPENSION SYSTEM

Interval • Lubricant
¼ **CG** Suspension system idler

CAUTION—Lubricate SUSPENSION SYS-
TEM POINTS on BOTH SIDES of TANK

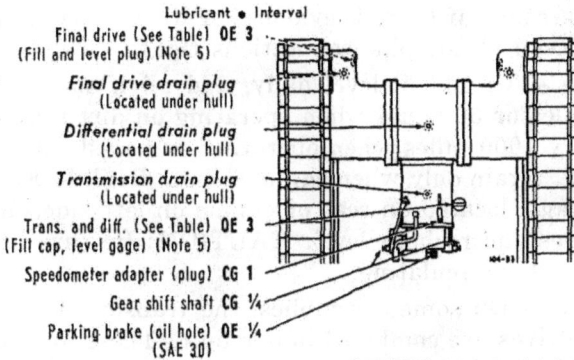

Lubricant • Interval
Final drive (See Table) **OE 3**
(Fill and level plug) (Note 5)

Final drive drain plug
(Located under hull)

Differential drain plug
(Located under hull)

Transmission drain plug
(Located under hull)

Trans. and diff. (See Table) **OE 3**
(Fill cap, level gage) (Note 5)

Speedometer adapter (plug) **CG 1**

Gear shift shaft **CG ¼**

Parking brake (oil hole) **OE ¼**
(SAE 30)

TRANSMISSION,
DIFFERENTIAL AND
FINAL DRIVES
(3-piece unit)
See Reverse Side for other
type construction

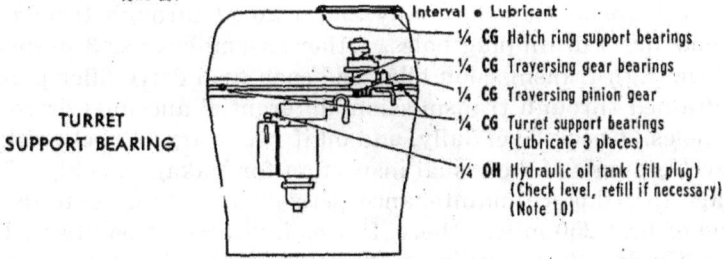

Interval • Lubricant

¼ **CG** Hatch ring support bearings

¼ **CG** Traversing gear bearings

¼ **CG** Traversing pinion gear

¼ **CG** Turret support bearings
(Lubricate 3 places)

¼ **OH** Hydraulic oil tank (fill plug)
(Check level, refill if necessary)
(Note 10)

TURRET
SUPPORT BEARING

——— **KEY** ———

LUBRICANTS	INTERVALS
OE—OIL, engine **OH**—OIL, hydraulic **CG**—GREASE, general purpose No. 1 (above +32°) No. 1 or No. 0 (+32° to +10°) No. 0 (below +10°)	¼— 250 MILES 1—1,000 MILES 3—3,000 MILES

Preliminary lubrication instructions based on Pilot model only.

RA PD 27243

Figure 9 — Lubrication Chart on Suspension

25

adapters until grease overflows relief valve. Lubricate other fittings until new grease is forced from the bearing, unless otherwise specified. CAUTION: Lubricate suspension points after washing tank.

2. INTERVALS — The intervals indicated at points on Lubrication Guide are for normal service. For extreme conditions of speed, heat, water, mud, snow, rough roads, dust, etc., reduce interval on guide by $\frac{1}{3}$ or $\frac{1}{2}$, or more if conditions warrant.

3. AIR CLEANERS — Proper maintenance of air cleaners is essential to prolonged engine life. Drain, clean and refill with OIL, engine, crankcase grade, daily, when operating on dirt roads or cross country; every 250 miles when operating on paved roads or during wet weather. Depending on operating conditions, remove air cleaners and wash all parts every 100 to 500 miles. Inspect air outlet rubber hose connections for leaks and make sure pipes are in alinement. Replace connections if there is evidence of wear or deterioration. CAUTION: Keep all air pipe connections tight.

4. CRANKCASE — Check oil level daily, add oil if necessary. Drain every 500 miles or 50 hours when operating on dirt roads or cross country; every 1000 miles when operating on paved roads or during wet weather. Drain only when engine is hot. Refill to FULL mark on bayonet gage, located on rear of engine on left side. Run engine a few minutes and recheck level. CAUTION: Be sure pressure gage indicates oil is circulating.

5. GEAR CASES — On some assemblies, the transmission, differential and final drives are combined in one unit. These are filled through transmission filler only and drained through transmission and final drive drain plug holes. Other assemblies use 3-piece units, filled through transmission filler and each final drive filler plug hole and drained through transmission, differential and final drive drain plug holes. Check level daily, add oil if necessary. Check with tank on level ground. Make visual inspection for leakage weekly. Report leakage to ordnance maintenance personnel. Drain, flush and refill at end of first 250 miles; thereafter as indicated at points on Lubrication Guide. When draining, drain immediately after operation. To flush cases, fill to proper level with OIL, engine, SAE 10. Operate tank slowly in low gear for several minutes and redrain. Fill gear cases with OIL, engine, grade specified in table of capacities and recommendations. CAUTION: Fill single piece unit to mark on bayonet gage with fill cap resting on top of fill pipe. Fill 3-piece unit to 1 inch below final drive fill plug holes and to mark on transmission bayonet gage. Clean transmission filler strainer every 3000 miles. CAUTION: Do not remove strainer when filling.

6. AUXILIARY GENERATOR — Two-cycled air cooled engine, mounted on turret floor, rear, is lubricated by OIL, engine, with fuel.

Mix thoroughly ⅜ pint OIL, engine, SAE 30, with each gallon of gasoline before pouring into tank. CAUTION: Do not pour gasoline and oil separately into tank. Keep fuel strainer clean. Magneto — Every 200 hours, lubricate magneto cam follower by oiling felt with one or two drops OIL, engine, SAE 30.

7. FUEL FILTER — Open drain cock daily to remove sediment and water. Every 1000 miles, remove element and wash in fuel or SOLVENT, dry-cleaning.

8. UNIVERSAL JOINTS AND SLIP JOINT — Remove tunnel shield sections over universal joints and slip joint at ends of tunnel shield. Lubricate universal joints through fittings with GREASE, general purpose, seasonal grade, until grease overflows at relief valve. To lubricate slip joint, remove plug and insert fitting. Apply GREASE, general purpose, seasonal grade, until grease is forced from end of spline. CAUTION: After lubricating, remove fitting and replace plug.

9. OIL FILTER — The oil filter is of the self-turning type and is located in the engine crankcase. Remove filter from crankcase every 1000 miles, drain sediment from housing and reinstall.

10. HYDRAULIC OIL TANK — Located on side of turret. Check level every 250 miles by means of glass level gage. Add OIL, hydraulic, if necessary. Drain, flush and refill every six months. Capacity 12 quarts.

11. OIL CAN POINTS — Lubricate machine gun mount ball socket, door and shield hinges, peep hole protector slides, door latches, lever bushings, control rod pins and clevises with OIL, engine, SAE 30, every 250 miles.

12. POINTS REQUIRING NO LUBRICATION — Water pump, clutch pilot bearing, clutch yoke bearing, clutch release bearing, fan hubs, bogie wheel suspension linkage, final drive sprocket bearings.

Section V

INSPECTIONS

17. PURPOSE.

a. To insure mechanical efficiency, it is necessary that tanks be systematically inspected at intervals in order that defects may be discovered and corrected before they result in serious damage.

b. Cracks that develop in castings or other metal parts may often be detected through the medium of dust and oil deposits upon the completion of the run.

c. Suggestions toward changes in design prompted by chronic failure or malfunction of a unit or group of units; pertinent changes in inspection or maintenance methods; and changes involving safety, efficiency, economy, and comfort should be forwarded to the Office of the Chief of Ordnance, through proper channels, at the time they develop. Such action is encouraged, in order that other organizations may profit thereby.

18. PRESTARTING INSPECTION.

The tank has a crew of five men and it is essential that all men be utilized in inspection of the tank under the direction of the tank commander. The inspection should cover the vehicle as well as the engine. During all inspections as a first operation elevate the gun so that it will not hurt anyone who may happen to have their head out of the front hatches at the same time someone else traverses the turret.

a. Elevate the 75-mm gun.

b. Look at the ground under the tank for oil and fuel leaks.

c. Check that all pioneer tools are present.

d. Check general condition of sprockets, bogies, springs, guides, gudgeons, track supporting rollers and idlers.

e. Check the track for wear, tightness and tension, and end connections for wear.

f. Check for tightness and wear of wedges and wedge nuts.

INSPECTIONS

g. Check for loose air horn connections from the carburetors to air cleaners.

h. Check fuel level, fill if necessary.

i. Check radio antenna for breaks.

j. Check transmission oil level with bayonet gage on right side of transmission, fill if necessary. Do not overfill, otherwise overheating will result.

k. Check for oil and fuel leaks on floor of fighting compartment.

l. Check for presence and condition of fire extinguishers, and tank tools.

m. Check instrument panel and see that voltmeter reads 16 with battery switch open and other instruments indicate normal shut-off readings.

n. Check that steering levers, clutch pedal and gear shift lever operate freely and over the full range.

o. Close battery switch and watch the ammeter and voltmeter. The voltmeter should read 24 or more volts. If ammeter shows excessive discharge, open the battery switch immediately.

p. Check to see that fuel valves are open.

q. Check lights and siren.

r. Check operation of turret and locking mechanism.

s. Check traverse and elevation of vehicle's weapons.

t. Check to see that ammunition, flags, field equipment and rations if carried, are properly loaded.

19. INSPECTION DURING OPERATION.

a. During operation the driver will be on the alert to detect abnormal functioning of the engine. He should be trained to detect unusual engine sounds or noises. He should glance frequently at the instrument panel gages to see if the engine is functioning properly. An unsteady oil gage needle indicates low oil pressure, provided that engine speed is fairly constant. The driver should notice continuously the amount of free play or clearance of the clutch pedal which should be at least two inches. The steering mechanism must be checked for: clearance before engagement, intensity of pull required for braking, etc.

b. Only under exceptional circumstances will a tank be operated after indications of trouble have been observed. When in doubt, the engine will be stopped, and assistance obtained. Inspection during operation applies to the entire vehicle and should be emphasized throughout the driving instruction period.

20. INSPECTION AT THE HALT.

a. At each halt the operator will make a careful inspection of the tank to determine its general mechanical condition. Minor defects detected during the march, together with defects discovered at the halt, will be corrected before resuming the march. If the defects cannot be corrected during the halt, proper disposition of the vehicle will be made so that unnecessary delay may be avoided and a major failure prevented.

b. A suitable general routine is as follows:

(1) Elevate the 75-mm gun.

(2) By means of the ignition switch, cut out in turn each bank of cylinders to make sure all cylinders are firing. Allow the engine to run a short time on both magnetos at idling speed (500 rpm). Listen for unusual noises.

(3) Walk around the vehicle looking carefully for fuel or oil leaks.

(4) Examine tracks for adjustment and for worn, loose, broken or missing parts.

(5) Inspect hull and fittings for missing, worn, or loose parts.

(6) Feel steering brake housings and gear case for evidence of overheating. If abnormally hot, check level or lubricant and if necessary correct steering brake band adjustment.

(7) Inspect the lights, if traveling at night with lights.

(8) Check the amount of fuel in the tank.

(9) Wipe all windshield and vision devices. Do not use an oily or dirty cloth.

21. INSPECTION AFTER OPERATION.

At the conclusion of each day's operation, the tank commander should cause an inspection to be made, similar to that made at halts but more thorough and detailed. The inspection should be followed by preventative maintenance. If defects cannot be corrected, they should be reported promptly to the chief of section or other designated individual. The following points should be covered:

a. Elevate the 75-mm gun.

b. Examine the tracks and bogies.

c. Check track tension.

d. Inspect idler track support rollers.

e. Examine the drive sprockets for worn or broken teeth.

f. Examine the track shoe units for unserviceable units.

g. Check transmission oil level.

h. Check, clean and refill air cleaners during extremely dusty operations.

i. Clean crankcase breather.

j. Inspect lights, siren and windshield wipers. Check for loss or damage of accessories.

k. Inspect the sighting and vision devices for breakage.

l. Inspect guns and mounts for defective performance.

m. Inspect guns, sighting equipment, and accessories and determine that covers are properly installed.

n. Inspect ammunition and sighting compartments for cleanliness and orderly arrangement.

o. Replenish ammunition, engine oil and fuel. Always touch the nozzle of the gasoline hose to the hull of the tank before removing gas tank cap to eliminate possibility of a static charge of electricity in either the tank or the gasoline truck from causing an explosion and fire when cap is removed from gas tanks. Don't fill the fuel tanks all the way; leave air space of approximately three gallons in each tank for fuel expansion.

p. For continuous operation in hot weather, battery water must be replenished about twice a week. Check and clean battery and compartment by removal of battery weekly.

q. Drain and clean all floors through spring loaded valves provided, being sure to remove any accumulation from the engine compartment—this is important to eliminate fire hazard.

r. Check the operation of the full flow oil filters. Reverse the manual turning nut on the rotating spindle at the hydraulic motor housing cover and crank the engine. The manual turning nut will rotate if the filter is operative.

s. Inspect all control linkage to locate loose or broken parts.

t. Inspect electrical wiring for loose connections.

u. Check to see that the fuel shut-off valves are closed.

v. Check to see that the battery switch is open.

22. PERIODIC INSPECTION.

a. After 250 miles of operation. This check is made without removing the engine from vehicle. (Check for leaks, etc., will be made with engine compartment open and engine running.) Make routine daily inspection and the following:

(1) Elevate the 75-mm gun.

(2) Inspection for oil leaks at oil pan.

(3) Check gasoline and oil lines for breaks, loose connections, and chafing. Check level of fuel in carburetor float bowl. Make external inspection of rigid and flexible lines having sharp bends or kinks.

(4) Remove the bolt passing through the fuel filter and remove and clean the bowl and filter element. If excessive water or dirt is observed, drain and clean fuel tanks.

(5) Service air cleaner, do not overfill with oil. Check all air induction pipes and air horn for leaks. Check carburetor flange gasket.

MEDIUM TANK M4A3

(6) Check and adjust all control linkage for wear, free operation and missing cotter pins. See that full travel of controls is obtained. This applies to all controls of the vehicle.

(7) Check all flexible conduits for breaks and worn sections.

(8) Tighten all engine mounting bolts.

(9) Check bogie, gudgeon nuts, wedges, wedge nuts, cotter pins and lock wire for tightness or broken and missing parts.

(10) Check propeller shaft flange nuts for tightness. .

(11) Check engine for excessive roughness.

(12) Check suspension for track tension, bogie wheel tires, volute springs and presence of foreign material.

(13) Change engine oil.

(14) Check oil level in transmission.

(15) Service battery.

(16) Check solenoids for operation.

(17) Check all accessories for security and operation.

(18) Road test for proper operation.

(19) Inspect fuel pump and, if leaking, notify ordnance personnel.

b. **After 1000 miles of operation.** Daily and 250 mile check will be repeated and the following in addition:

(1) Elevate 75-mm gun.

(2) Remove engine and place on inspection stand and clean with SOLVENT, cleaning.

(3) Disassemble clutch, inspect plates, lubricate clutch hub, spindle and throw-out bearings.

(4) Check clutch throw-out bearing for wear and flat spots on races.

(5) Check all exhaust pipes for cracks, burned out spots and rust.

(6) Check intake manifold gaskets and secure nuts for tightness.

(7) Remove radiators, clean all dirt in air passages, drain and flush out inside, completely removing flushing material.

(8) Change all spark plugs. Check new plugs. NOTE: Do not install spark plugs until all other top cylinder work has been completed.

(9) Check flywheel cap screws for tightness and presence of locking wire.

(10) Inspect magneto breaker and reset points to 0.014 to 0.016 inch using feeler gage. Check points for pitting. If points show ash colored burning, have condensers checked.

(11) Inspect carburetor for float bowl fuel level.

(12) Inspect starter and generator and brushes, commutator and general internal appearance. If brushes need replacing or if other repairs are indicated, replace starter or generator.

INSPECTIONS

(13) Check all nuts securing engine accessories, fan and shroud, support brackets, etc., for tightness.

(14) Check throttle rod at clevises for loose jam nuts and cracks at welds.

(15) Check foot accelerator to make sure both carburetors are wide open when foot throttle comes against stop.

(16) Check air horn rubber connections for restricted passages.

(17) Clean magnetic plugs in transmission and check magnetic ability.

(18) Check transmission oil.

(19) Lubricate vehicle throughout in compliance with lubrication instructions.

(20) Check and blow out fire extinguisher lines.

(21) Check and, where necessary, replace or exchange unit accessories such as headlights, batteries, sirens, generators, wiring harness, etc.

(22) Check, repair and adjust tracks.

(23) Road test.

MEDIUM TANK M4A3

Section VI

POWER UNIT AND ACCESSORIES

23. GENERAL DESCRIPTION AND DATA (figs. 10, 11, 12, and 13).

a. A 60 degree "V" 8-cylinder, 4-cycle, valve in the head, liquid cooled Ford tank engine is used. The cylinder block and crankcase are a single casting of aluminum with oil hardened steel dry type sleeves in cylinder bores. The water jackets extend the full length of cylinders which tends to speed up the warming of the engine oil in cold weather and to cool the oil after normal operating temperatures are reached. Four overhead camshafts are used, one exhaust and one intake for each bank of cylinders. There are two exhaust and two intake valves in each cylinder.

b. The engine is mounted at the rear of the tank and supported by four brackets, the two front brackets are mounted on the bulkhead in the tank body; the two rear brackets are mounted on the floor of the tank; rubber mounting is used between the brackets and the engine.

c. Two four cylinder magnetos are used. These are located at the rear of the engine, one mounted at each end of a cross shaft driven by spiral gears. The water pump is driven from the end of the crankshaft. The two pusher type fans are driven by double belts from accessory drives located on the wall of the tank. The generator is driven by the opposite end of the fan accessory shaft.

A—OIL FILTER
B—OIL FILLER PIPE
C—MOUNT
D—HUB
E—MANIFOLD, EXHAUST
F—TUBE, EXHAUST
G—MANIFOLD, CARBURETOR
H—MANIFOLD, WATER
J—COVER
K—TUBE, EXHAUST
L—HEAD
M—MOUNT
N—MOTOR, STARTER
P—BLOCK
Q—OIL PAN

RA PD 27200

Figure 10 — Right Side of Engine

MEDIUM TANK M4A3

A—MOUNT
B—TUBE, EXHAUST
C—COVER
D—MANIFOLD, CARBURETOR
E—MANIFOLD, WATER
F—HEAD

G—HUB
H—MOUNT
J—OIL PAN
K—GAUGE UNIT
L—MANIFOLD, EXHAUST
M—BLOCK

RA PD 27201

Figure 11 —Left Side of Engine

POWER UNIT AND ACCESSORIES

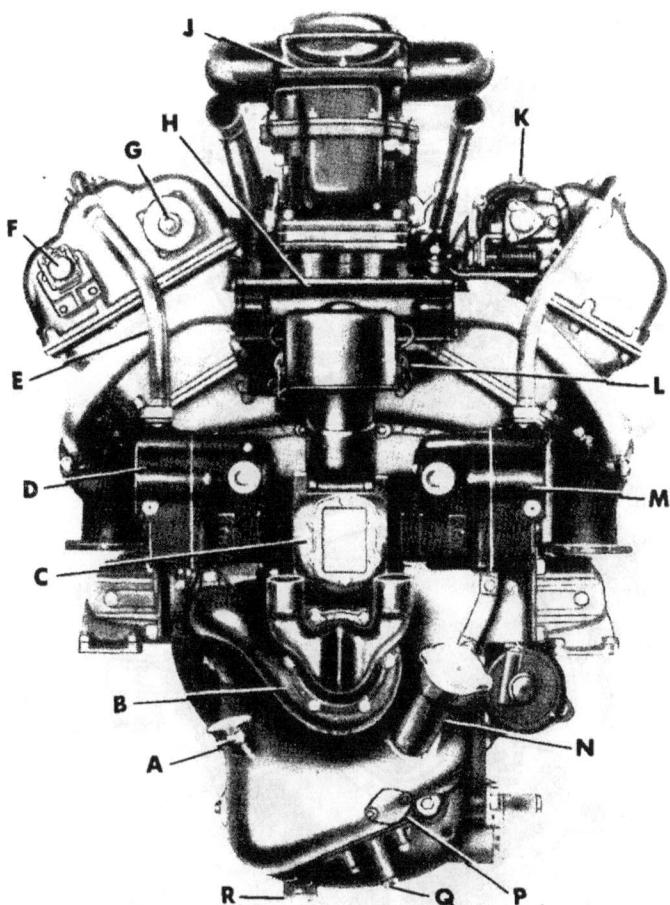

A—INDICATOR
B—PUMP, WATER
C—COVER
D—MAGNETO
E—CONDUIT
F—REVOLUTION COUNTER
G—TACHOMETER
H—ADAPTER
J—CARBURETOR

K—GOVERNOR
L—FILTER
M—MAGNETO
N—OIL FILLER PIPE
P—COVER
Q—OIL PUMP
R—PLUG

RA PD 27203

Figure 12 — Rear View of Engine

MEDIUM TANK M4A3

A—HOUSING
B—COVER
C—HEAD
D—COVER
E—CARBURETOR

F—ADAPTER
G—BLOCK
H—FLANGE
J—NUT
K—FORK

RA PD 27202

Figure 13 — Front View of Engine

POWER UNIT AND ACCESSORIES

The oil pump (gear type) is driven direct from the end of the vertical cam drive shaft.

d. The flywheel end of engine will be referred to as the "front" of the engine as the unit is mounted in the tank with the flywheel forward. The terms "right" and "left" are used with reference to the engine as viewed from the rear looking toward front of the tank.

e. The following data include the general information and engine characteristics which are frequently required for reference:

Make and type....................Ford "V" 8-cylinder tank engine
Model ....GAA
Over-all dimensions...60.38-in. long
33.25-in. wide
41.56-in. high
Weight ....1470 lbs
Horsepower ....500 at 2600 rpm
Number of cylinders...8
Bore ....5.4-in.
Stroke ....6-in.
Piston displacement..1100 cu in.
Compression ratio..7.5 to 1

Direction of rotation (viewed from rear of engine):

Crankshaft ....Clockwise
Starter ....Anticlockwise
Magnetos {Right hand ....Clockwise
{Left hand ....Anticlockwise

Accessory speeds:

Tachometer ....½ Crankshaft speed
Generator ....1.73 to Crankshaft speed
Magneto ....½ Crankshaft speed

Magneto:

Make and model.............................Bosch MJF-4A308
Breaker point gap........................0.014-in.-0.016-in.
Spark plug gap...........................0.011-in.-0.014-in.

Valve clearance (non-adjustable)..................0.023-in.-0.028-in.
Carburetor—make and model (2 used)....Bendix Stromberg NA-45G

Numbering of cylinders from rear to front:

Right bank 1-2-3-4
Left bank 1-2-3-4

Firing order......................1-R 2-L 3-R 1-L 4-R 3-L 2-R 4-L

24. ENGINE TROUBLE SHOOTING.

a. **If the engine fails to turn over when starter button is pressed:**

(1) Check the specific gravity of the batteries. If reading is 1.225 or less, replace with a fully charged battery and have the discharged battery recharged. If reading is approximately 1.280 the battery is fully charged.

(2) Examine battery terminals for corrosion, battery cable for a short circuit or broken sections. If such conditions exist, clean the terminals and replace the broken cables.

(3) Examine for loose connection at starter motor.

(4) Press the starter button to determine if the starter solenoid is working. Disconnect the battery-starter motor cable at the starter motor, and while another person operates the starter button, hold the cable against the housing and observe whether a spark occurs. If no spark is seen, replace the solenoid. If the starter does not operate after replacing solenoid, replace the starter.

b. **If the engine turns over but does not start.**

(1) See that ignition switch is turned "on."

(2) Check the amount of fuel in fuel tanks, and be sure the fuel valves are open.

(3) Under priming or over priming. For under prime reprime engine with two or three additional strokes. For over prime place throttle in full open position and turn engine over with starter five or six revolutions with magneto switch in "off" position.

(4) Check fuel level in carburetors by removing float chamber level plugs (see fig. 14). If fuel is not apparent at the carburetor levels, disconnect the inlet lines to carburetors and crank engine with starting motor. If no fuel flows, remove fuel pump outlet lines and blow out with air hose.

(5) After it has been determined that fuel is being supplied to carburetors the ignition system should be checked as follows: Remove circular distributor plate from right hand magneto and hold neon spark plug tester against each of the four high tension terminals in turn while engine is being cranked with the starter. A bright flash will show that the magneto, spark plugs and wire from that terminal is operating satisfactorily. If dim light shows, check wire and spark plug. Follow same procedure with left hand magneto. If the neon tester is not available the test may be made as follows: Remove the spark plug lead from the spark plug to be tested and hold it approximately ¼ inch away from a suitable ground connection. Turn the engine over with the starting motor and if a good spark is noticed the circuit is in good condition. Test the other

POWER UNIT AND ACCESSORIES

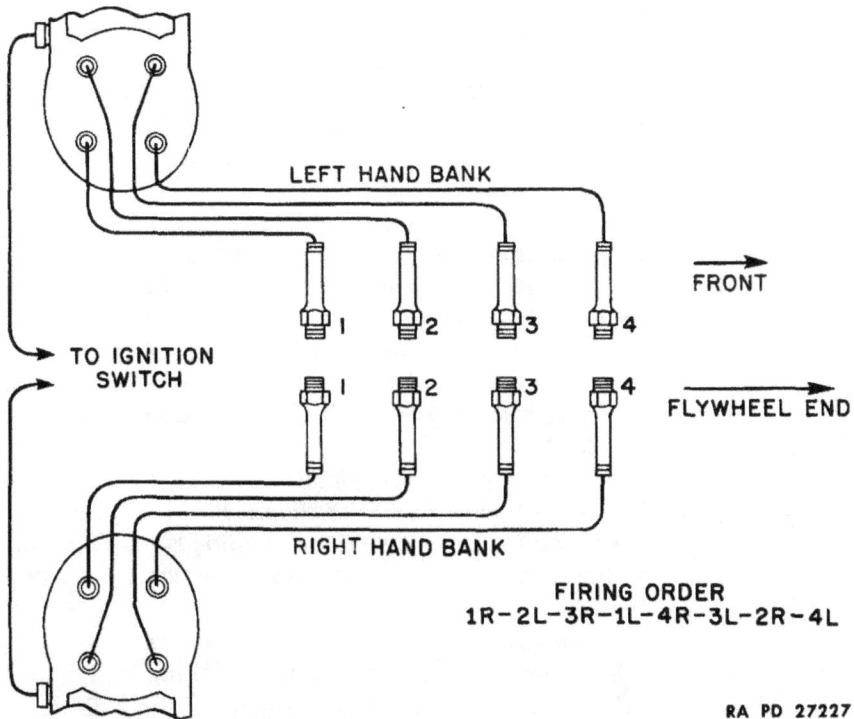

Figure 14 — Engine Firing Order

spark plugs in the same manner. If testing in the bright sunlight the spark should be shielded so that it can be seen. If test shows that either of the magnetos are not operating, replace.

(6) If the engine still will not start notify ordnance personnel.

c. **If the engine runs unevenly.**

(1) **Poor fuel mixture.** Too rich a mixture is evidenced by uneven running and black smoke from the exhaust. Too lean is evidenced by uneven running, overheating, or back-firing through the carburetor.

(2) **Leaks in induction system.** Examine carburetor intake manifold flanges for tightness. Also examine carburetor gaskets.

(3) **Ignition trouble.** In case of defective ignition, it must first be determined whether the fault is in the right or left bank. This can be determined by running first on the right bank and then on the left bank by means of the ignition switch. In general, when only one cylinder misfires, the fault is in the spark plug. The most common plug difficulties are as follows:

(a) **Plug gap too wide.** The distance between the electrodes of the spark plug should be 0.011-inch to 0.014-inch. Too wide a gap increases the electrical resistance and interferes with the operation of the engine.

(b) **Plug short-circuited.** This is usually caused by a cracked or porous insulator, or by fouling of the electrodes or insulator. Any of these conditions will cause misfiring by permitting the current to stray from its intended path.

(c) **Ignition wires.** Misfiring of one cylinder, either continuous or intermittent, may be due also to a chafed or broken wire. The metal terminals of the cables must not come into contact with any metal parts of the engine or the magneto, except those designated as being correct according to the instructions given. If the wires and plugs are in good condition and yet the ignition is irregular, the trouble is probably with the magneto. This can be checked as outlined in paragraph 25, **b.**

(d) **Damaged insulating parts.** It sometimes happens that distributor plate and control arm cap parts of the magneto are damaged through accident or carelessness. These parts should also be carefully examined for possible disarrangement or damage which might permit leakage of current.

(4) **Valve and valve gear trouble.** Check the valve clearances, and the springs. Make sure the valves are not sticking.

(5) **Poor fuel.** Use only the recommended grade of gasoline and see that it flows freely to the carburetor.

(6) **Engine overheating.** Excessive engine temperature may be due to any of the following causes:

(a) Air flow restricted through radiator.

(b) Engine operating on too lean a fuel mixture.

(c) Engine operating on a retarded spark.

(d) Engine oil of improper grade, of insufficient quantity.

25. MAGNETOS.

a. **Description.** Two magnetos are used, one firing the cylinders in the right block and the other firing the cylinders in the left block. The right or left block is determined by looking at the engine from the rear of the tank, looking toward the front. The numbering of the cylinders and the firing order is shown in figure 14. The wires leading from the magneto distributor to the spark plugs may be identified for both right and left hand magneto by colors marked on the wires as follows: No. 1 red, No. 2 blue, No. 3 green, and No. 4 yellow.

b. **Check ignition timing.**

(1) Open top engine compartment doors.

(2) Remove plate over spark plugs in each block and remove spark plug caps, wires and spark plugs.

POWER UNIT AND ACCESSORIES

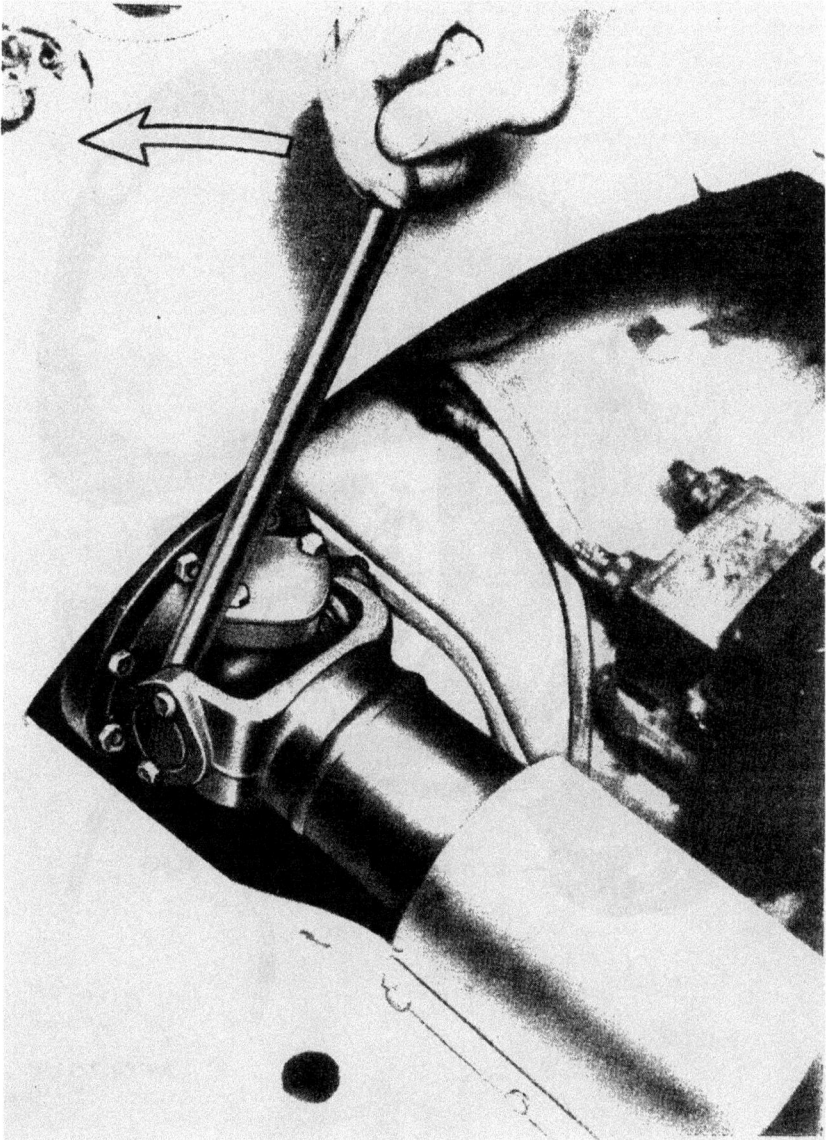

RA PD 27238

Figure 15 — Turning Engine by Hand

MEDIUM TANK M4A3

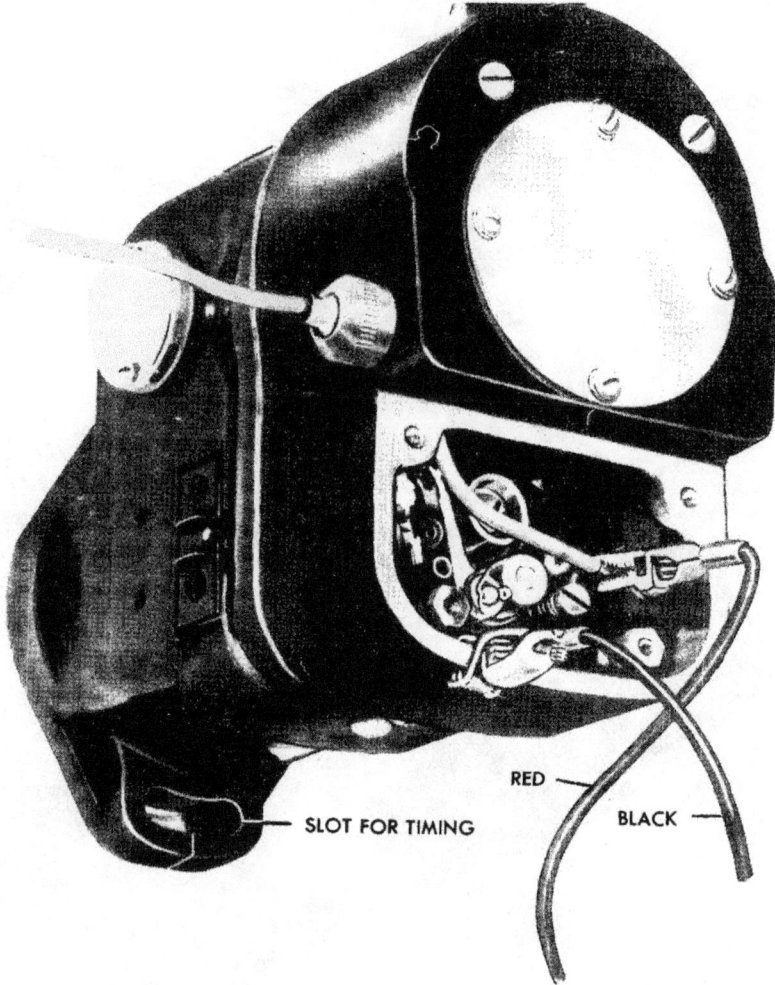

SLOT FOR TIMING

RED

BLACK

RA PD 27235

Figure 16 — Connections for Magneto Timing Light

Figure 17 — Magneto Rotor Arrow   RA PD 27234

(3) Remove timing plate on flywheel housing in front of left block. To do this it is necessary to remove fire extinguisher nozzle between side of left block and wall of tank; also remove small "Homelite" muffler mounted on bulkhead.

(4) Remove cover over rear universal joint and use bar for turning engine as shown in figure 15. Use compression gage in No. 1 spark plug hole and turn engine counterclockwise or from right to left until compression gage shows No. 1 piston is coming up on compression stroke. Then turn until No. 1 cylinder right hand mark is approaching pointer in opening in flywheel housing.

(5) Remove magneto breaker point cover plates and connect one of the red wires of the timing light to the primary connection of the right hand magneto, and the other red wire to the primary connection of the left hand magneto. Then ground the black wire to either magneto frame as shown in figure 16.

(6) One man should be in position to observe flywheel timing marks, and another to turn engine a small amount at a time. Place the ignition switch on instrument board on "R"; turn engine only a very small amount at a time until right indicator light goes "on" showing the breaker points have just opened.

(7) The flywheel mark "Spark Retarded" should be under the pointer (fig. 17).

c. **Ignition timing.**

(1) Should the flywheel mark be past the pointer when the timing light goes on, the timing is late, in which case it will be necessary to advance the magneto in the housing slots (fig. 17).

(2) Loosen the upper and lower holding nuts and move the magneto counterclockwise, slightly back up the flywheel to remove backlash and check again. (Clockwise or counterclockwise is looking at magnetos from coupling ends.)

(3) Tighten holding nuts after correct timing is obtained. NOTE: To time the left magneto, turn the engine approximately two revolutions before using the compression gage on No. 1 cylinder in the left cylinder block. Turn ignition switch to "L" and proceed the same as for right block.

d. **Magneto replacement.**

(1) **Removal**

(a) Remove the four screws securing the breaker point inspection plate and remove the plate.

(b) Remove the four screws securing the magneto distributor circular inspection plate; and remove the plate.

(c) Remove the screw holding the ground wire.

(d) Unscrew the knurled nut securing the ground wire conduit to the magneto housing, and remove the ground wire and conduit.

(e) Remove the four screws securing the four ignition (high tension) cables to the distributor plate and lift the ignition cables out of the recesses.

(f) Unscrew the knurled nut securing the ignition cable conduit to the magneto and remove the conduit and cables.

(g) Remove one upper and one lower nut securing the magneto to the timing gear case and remove the magneto.

(h) CAUTION: Note the position of the arrow in the center of the distributor plate before removing the magneto. The magneto must be replaced with the arrow pointing to the same terminal as when removed.

(2) **Installation.** Reverse the sequence of removal operations to install, and time the magneto in accordance with the procedure in paragraph 25 c.

26. SPARK PLUGS.

a. **Description.** The spark plugs used are the Aircraft type, Champion C88-S, and are radio shielded. The spark gap is 0.011-inch to 0.014-inch.

POWER UNIT AND ACCESSORIES

b. **Removal.**

(1) Remove plates over spark plug compartment, shield caps from spark plugs and spark plug wires.

(2) Remove spark plugs.

c. **Installation.** When installing spark plugs do not use a wrench with handle more than 10 inches long. It is possible to distort certain sections of the plug if too much force is used in tightening.

27. FUEL PUMP.

a. **Description.** The fuel pump is of the automotive diaphragm type (AC) and is mounted on left cylinder bank and is driven by left intake camshaft. The pump maintains a pressure of five pounds to the carburetor.

b. **Maintenance.** At the 250 mile inspection check for leakage at connections and fittings.

c. **Removal.** In the event the fuel pump fails to supply a sufficient quantity of fuel, the pump should be replaced with a serviceable unit. The following procedure should be followed:

(1) Close fuel shut-off valves.

(2) Disconnect fuel lines attached to pump. (Disconnect the pump to carburetor fuel lines at carburetor before attempting to remove from pump.)

(3) Remove the two nuts which hold the pump to cylinder head and remove the pump.

d. **Installation.** Proceed in reverse order given in paragraph 27 c.

28. CARBURETORS.

a. **Description.** Two Stromberg model NA-Y5G Carburetors are used, one mounted at each end of the intake manifold. The carburetor is a double barreled down-draft unit. It has two floats connected by one lever and operating one needle valve. A separate main metering and idling system is provided for each barrel. Each barrel is equipped with a vacuum operated degasser and an electrical control for positive shut-off of the fuel when stopping the engine. This is controlled by a toggle switch on the instrument panel, and is used in case the engine continues to turn over after the ignition switch is cut off due to preignition or faulty wiring.

b. **Idle adjustment.** The idle fuel adjusting screws are shown in figure 18. There is one for each carburetor barrel.

(1) Make idle fuel adjustments with engine stopped.

(2) Seat each idle fuel adjusting screw lightly, and then turn out each screw $\frac{1}{4}$ turn. There are two adjusting screws on each carburetor, one for each throttle barrel.

MEDIUM TANK M4A3

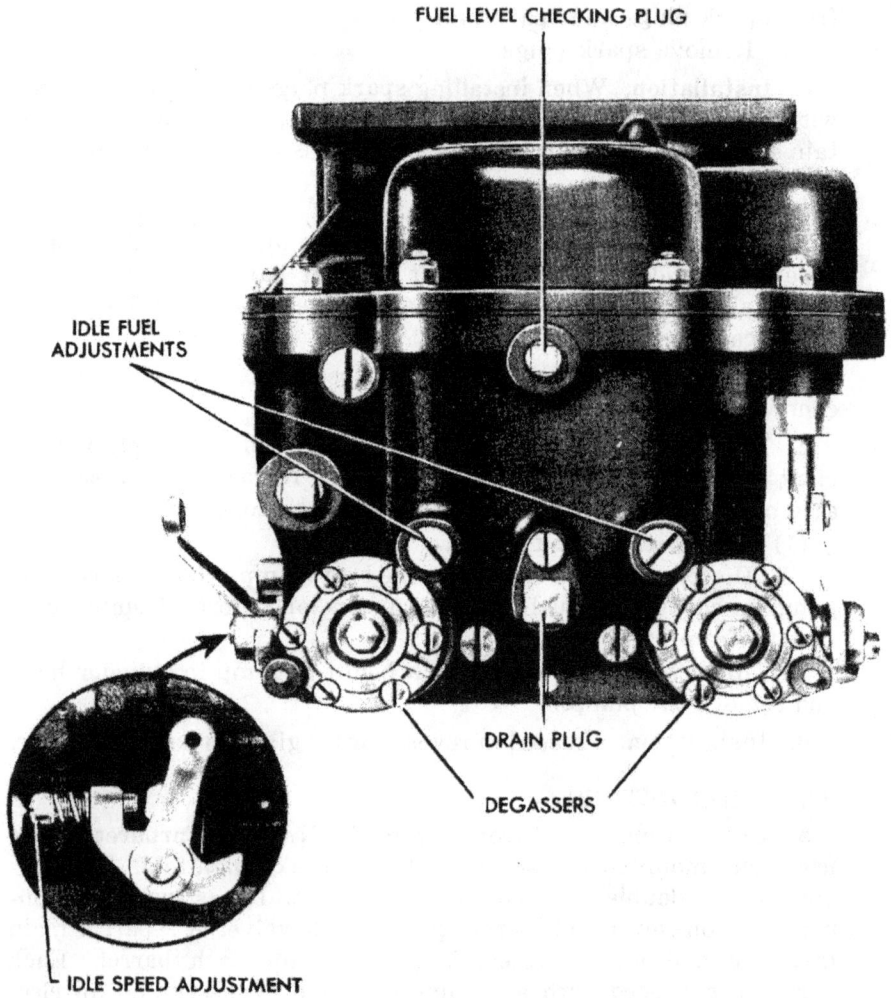

FUEL LEVEL CHECKING PLUG

IDLE FUEL
ADJUSTMENTS

DRAIN PLUG

DEGASSERS

IDLE SPEED ADJUSTMENT

RA PD 27233

Figure 18 — Carburetor

(3) Adjust idle speed adjusting screw so that it is ¼ turn open from closed position.

(4) Start the engine and run until it reaches normal operating temperature. After engine is warmed up set idle speed adjusting screw so that the engine idles at 500 rpm.

c. **Removal.** To remove carburetors proceed as follows:

(1) Remove the six nuts at the top of each carburetor which hold the air cleaner manifold.

(2) Disconnect the two air cleaner manifold hose pipes, by loosening the clamps and remove air cleaner manifold.

(3) Disconnect gas feed line at each carburetor. NOTE: A small cork should be available to cork the intake to prevent gasoline from running out when feed line is disconnected.

(4) Disconnect degasser electrical connections at each side of carburetor.

(5) Remove the four carburetor base nuts which hold the carburetor to the manifold.

(6) Disconnect throttle rod at each carburetor and remove the carburetors.

d. **Installation.** The carburetors may be replaced by reversing the procedure outlined above.

29. AIR CLEANERS.

a. **Description.** Two air cleaners of the oil bath type are located one at the right and one at the left of the fighting compartment mounted on the forward side of the bulkhead.

b. **Maintenance.** Daily or after every eight hours of operation in mild dust conditions, service the air cleaners as follows:

(1) **Daily servicing.** Turn turret until the door in the turret exposes the air cleaner. Remove the three wing nuts from the bottom plate of the cleaner, and remove the baffle and cup assembly. Remove the baffle from the cup and clean both baffle and cup thoroughly. Refill the cup to proper level with oil specified (see lubrication chart, Section IV). Care should be taken not to fill the cup over the oil level mark. Place the bottom plate on cleaner and fasten with the three wing nuts.

(2) **Cleaning filter element.** After 25 hours of normal engine operation, clean the filter element by first removing the baffle and cup assembly, and then removing the filter element by pulling the clip down. Wash filter elements with cleaning fluid or gasoline. Dry and blow out with compressed air in reverse direction to normal air travel.

c. Removal.

(1) Turn turret until door in turret exposes air cleaner.

(2) Disconnect rubber outlet connection to carburetor air intake manifold.

(3) Remove the cup from the cleaner.

(4) Remove four cap screws connecting cleaner to bulkhead.

(5) Lift out cleaner.

d. Installation. Reverse the sequence of removal operation.

30. GOVERNOR.

The governor is used to regulate and limit the speed of the engine, thus preventing dangerous over-speeding. The unit is located at the rear of right hand cylinder head. The governor is set to limit the engine speed to 2650 rpm under full load and should not be tampered with except by ordnance maintenance personnel.

31. VALVE MECHANISM.

Two inlet and two exhaust valves are provided for each cylinder and are operated by overhead camshafts, two in each cylinder head, one shaft operating the intake valves and the other operating the exhaust valves. Special non-adjustable tappets are used. The clearance of 0.023-inch to 0.028-inch is determined during manufacture, and should require no attention other than checking as both intake and exhaust valve ports are provided with steel inserts. The tappet clearance should remain constant over a long period of operation. In the event the clearance becomes too small, it will be necessary to grind off valve stem to obtain correct clearance.

32. MANIFOLDS.

a. Description. The intake manifold is cast in the cylinder head, and is open at each end where the front and rear carburetors are attached. Two exhaust manifolds are used and are bolted directly to right and left side of the block and connected to each other at the rear. Each exhaust manifold is connected to a separate exhaust pipe.

33. ENGINE REPLACEMENT.

a. Removal.

(1) Open the door at the rear of the engine compartment. To open this door all the way raise the radiator air baffle and allow it to rest on top of the door after the door is open.

(2) Remove plug in engine compartment floor plate.

(3) Open drain valve at bottom of water pump and drain through the hole in floor plate.

(4) Remove engine compartment floor plate.

(5) Drain engine oil pan.

(6) Remove the nuts securing water pump, disconnect the water pump hose and remove the water pump.

(7) Remove radiator top hose and two condenser tank hoses.

(8) Open the grilled engine compartment doors and remove the front and rear hatch plates.

(9) Disconnect fan belts on each side of engine by loosening accessory drive adjustments.

(10) Remove four bolts in each fan shroud.

(11) Remove fan assemblies from engine compartment.

(12) Turn off battery master switch.

(13) Disconnect starter lead at starter.

(14) Disconnect generator armature and generator field lead at generator.

(15) Disconnect oil level indicator on left side of the oil pan.

(16) Disconnect oil pressure lead at right rear of the crankcase.

(17) Disconnect two magneto ground wires at the magnetos.

(18) Disconnect degasser wires from carburetors and degasser conduit from engine.

(19) Disconnect the right and left accessory drive shafts from the respective accessory drive housings.

(20) Remove the accessory drive housings.

(21) Disconnect the tachometer from left cylinder head.

(22) Disconnect the clutch release rod at the clutch housing.

(23) Remove the circular spacer plate around the clutch housing.

(24) Shut off the fuel valves and disconnect the fuel line from the fuel pump.

(25) Disconnect throttle control rod.

(26) Disconnect air cleaner outlet pipes at the air cleaners.

(27) Disconnect driveshaft bolts at clutch shaft flange.

(28) Remove bolts securing the engine to the four support brackets.

(29) Disconnect exhaust pipe from exhaust manifold.

(30) Secure lifting sling to four engine lifting eyes.

(31) Remove engine from hull.

b. **Installation.** Reverse the sequence of removal operations.

34. STARTING MOTOR.

a. **Description.** The starting motor is a 24 volt type mounted on the right side of flywheel housing and its power is transmitted to the engine through an automatic drive. A solenoid switch located on right forward side of bulkhead closes the electrical circuit of the starting motor when the starter button on the instrument board is pressed. Rotation of the starter motor shaft causes the pinion of the automatic drive to advance and mesh with the flywheel. After the engine starts and the flywheel speed exceeds that of the starting motor, the pinion releases from the flywheel automatically. The starting motor bearings do not require lubricating.

b. **Removal.** Disconnect the two starter wires and remove three nuts which hold the starter motor to the crankcase flange and remove the starter.

c. **Installation.** Reverse above procedure. Refer to the wiring diagram, figure 19.

35. GENERATOR.

a. **Description.** A special Ford tank generator model GAA is used. The generator is 30 volt, 50 ampere capacity and current control is obtained by a generator regulator mounted underneath floor of turret. The generator is mounted on the accessory drive housing and driven by the accessory shaft.

b. **Lubrication.** Generators are properly lubricated at engine overhaul periods and should not require additional lubrication between overhaul periods.

c. **Removal.** A faulty generator should be replaced as follows:

(1) Turn off battery master switch.

(2) Disconnect wires from armature and field terminals.

(3) Disconnect flexible conduit.

(4) Remove the four nuts which hold the generator to accessory case and remove the generator.

d. **Installation.** Reverse procedure as outlined above. Refer to the wiring diagram, figure 19.

36. OIL PUMP.

a. **Description.** The oil pump is a gear type driven from the camshaft driveshaft. The oil pump should require no periodical check.

b. **Removal.** Remove engine compartment floor plate. Remove the four nuts holding the oil pump to the crankcase and remove the pump.

c. **Installation.** Secure the pump to the crankcase with the four nuts. Replace the engine compartment floor plate.

37. OIL FILTER.

a. **Description.** The oil filter is the motorized "Cuno" type located on the right side of the oil pan at the rear, accessible through the rear door.

POWER UNIT AND ACCESSORIES

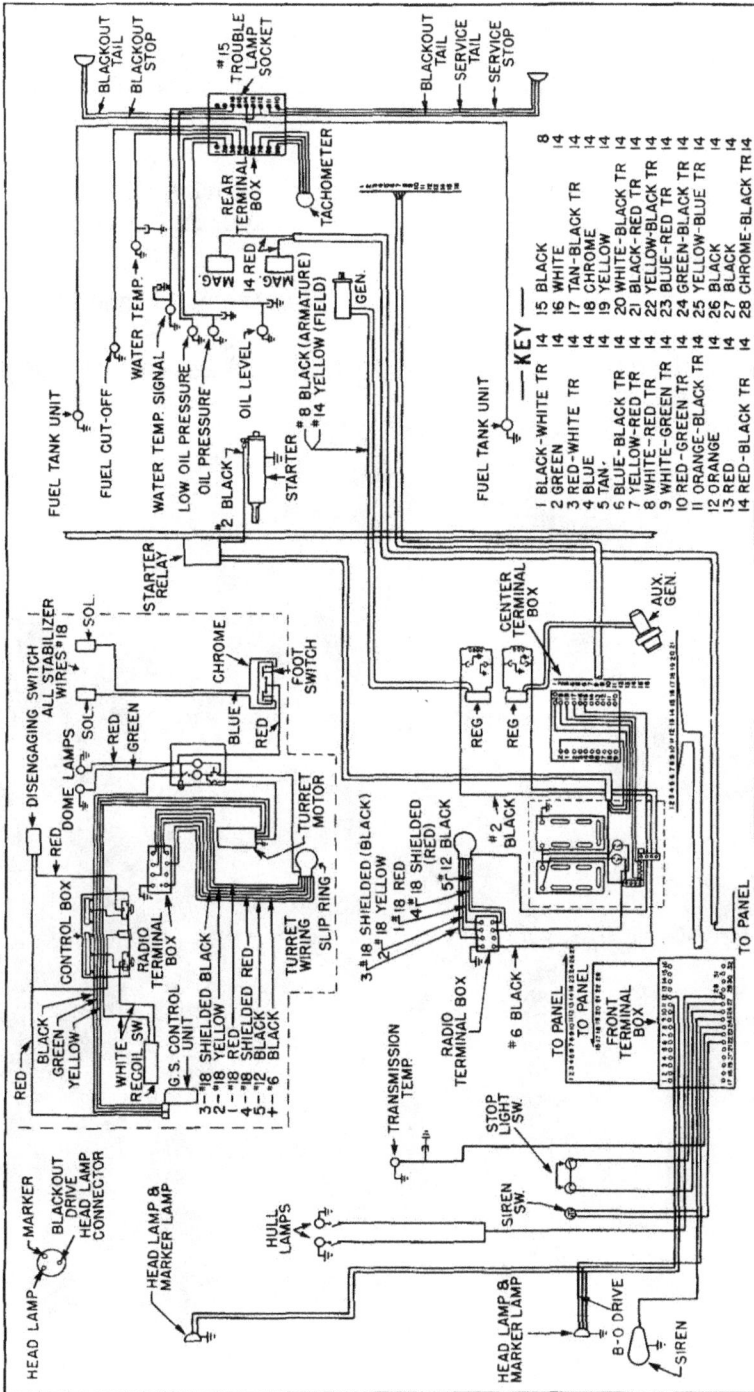

RA PD 27199

BLACKOUT TAIL
BLACKOUT STOP
#15 TROUBLE LAMP SOCKET
BLACKOUT TAIL
SERVICE TAIL
SERVICE STOP

REAR TERMINAL BOX
TACHOMETER
MAG.
14 RED
MAG.

WATER TEMP.
WATER TEMP. SIGNAL
LOW OIL PRESSURE
OIL PRESSURE
OIL LEVEL
GEN.
#8 BLACK (ARMATURE)
#14 YELLOW (FIELD)
STARTER
#2 BLACK

FUEL CUT-OFF
FUEL TANK UNIT
FUEL TANK UNIT

KEY

1 BLACK-WHITE TR 14
2 GREEN 14
3 RED-WHITE TR 14
4 BLUE 14
5 TAN 14
6 BLUE-BLACK TR 14
7 YELLOW-RED TR 14
8 WHITE-RED TR 14
9 WHITE-GREEN TR 14
10 RED-GREEN TR 14
11 ORANGE-BLACK TR 14
12 ORANGE 14
13 RED 14
14 RED-BLACK TR 14

15 BLACK 8
16 WHITE 14
17 TAN-BLACK TR 14
18 CHROME 14
19 YELLOW 14
20 WHITE-BLACK TR 14
21 BLACK-RED TR 14
22 YELLOW-BLACK TR 14
23 BLUE-RED TR 14
24 GREEN-BLACK TR 14
25 YELLOW-BLUE TR 14
26 BLACK 14
27 BLACK 14
28 CHROME-BLACK TR 14

STARTER RELAY

DISENGAGING SWITCH
ALL STABILIZER WIRES #18
SOL.
CHROME
FOOT SWITCH
SOL.
RED
GREEN
BLUE
RED
DOME LAMPS
RED
TURRET MOTOR
SLIP RING 3
CENTER TERMINAL BOX
AUX. GEN.
REG
REG

CONTROL BOX
RADIO TERMINAL BOX
TURRET WIRING

RED
BLACK
GREEN
YELLOW
WHITE
RECOIL SW.
G.S. CONTROL UNIT

3—#18 SHIELDED BLACK
2—#18 YELLOW
1—#18 RED
4—#18 SHIELDED RED
5—#12 BLACK
+—#6 BLACK

3 #18 SHIELDED (BLACK)
#18 RED
1 #18 YELLOW
4 #18 SHIELDED (RED)
5 #12 BLACK
#2 BLACK

RADIO TERMINAL BOX
#6 BLACK
#2 BLACK

TO PANEL
TO PANEL
FRONT TERMINAL BOX
TO PANEL

MARKER
BLACKOUT DRIVE
HEAD LAMP CONNECTOR
HEAD LAMP
HEAD LAMP & MARKER LAMP

TRANSMISSION TEMP.
STOP LIGHT SW.
HULL LAMPS
SIREN SW.
HEAD LAMP & MARKER LAMP
B-O DRIVE
SIREN

Figure 19 — Wiring Diagram

MEDIUM TANK M4A3

b. Operation check. To check the operation of the filter, reverse the manual turning nut, and turn the engine over with the starter. The manual turning nut will rotate if the filter is operating. After the check is made, replace the manual turning nut in original position and secure with lock wire.

c. Removal. Unscrew the six cap screws securing the motor and filter element to the crankcase, and remove motor and filter element.

d. Installation

(1) Clean the filter body before installing the motor and filtering element.

(2) Replace the motor and filter element and secure with the six cap screws.

Section VII

REFERENCES

38. STANDARD NOMENCLATURE LISTS.

Gun, cal. .30, Browning, M1919A4, fixed and flexible bow
   mounts .... SNL A-6
Gun, sub-machine, cal. .45, Thompson, M1928A1............ SNL A-32
Gun, machine, cal. .50, Browning, M2, heavy barrel, fixed
   and flexible and ground mounts.......................... SNL A-39
Materiel, 75-mm, tank gun, M2, M3......................... SNL C-34
Tank, medium, M4A2 (in preparation)..................... SNL G-104
                                          Vol. VIII

39. TECHNICAL AND FIELD MANUALS.

75-mm tank gun materiel.................................... TM 9-307
Cleaning, preserving, and lubricating materials.............. TM 9-850
Browning machine gun, cal. .50, all types.................... TM 9-1225
Stabilizers, all types....................................... TM 9-1799
Fire prevention, safety precautions, accidents............... TM 10-360
Sheet metal work, body, fender and radiator repairs...... TM 10-450
Echelon system of maintenance.............................. TM 10-525
Automotive lubrication .... TM 10-540
Motor transport inspection................................. TM 10-545
Automotive electricity .... TM 10-580
Defense against chemical attack............................ FM 21-40
Gun, sub-machine, cal. .45, Thompson, M1928A1.......... FM 23-40
Gun, cal. .30, Browning, M1919A4.......................... FM 23-50

40. MISCELLANEOUS PUBLICATIONS.

Military motor vehicles..................................... AR 850-15
Storage of motor vehicle equipment......................... AR 850-18
Detailed lubrication instructions for ordnance
   materiel ....OFSB 6 Series

INDEX

INDEX

MEDIUM TANK M4A3

INDEX

INDEX

MEDIUM TANK M4A3

[A. G. 062.11 (8-4-42)]

By order of the Secretary of War:

G. C. MARSHALL,
Chief of Staff.

Official:

J. A. ULIO,
Major General,
The Adjutant General.

DISTRIBUTION: D 17 (10); IR 17 (6), 9(2); IBn 9(1), 17(4); IC 17 (17), 9(3)

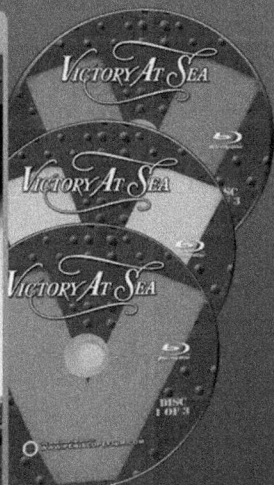

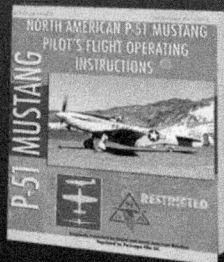

www.ingramcontent.com/pod-product-compliance
Lightning Source LLC
Chambersburg PA
CBHW060147050426
42448CB00010B/2342